Kawika guillermo

nimrods

ANTI-
MEMOIR

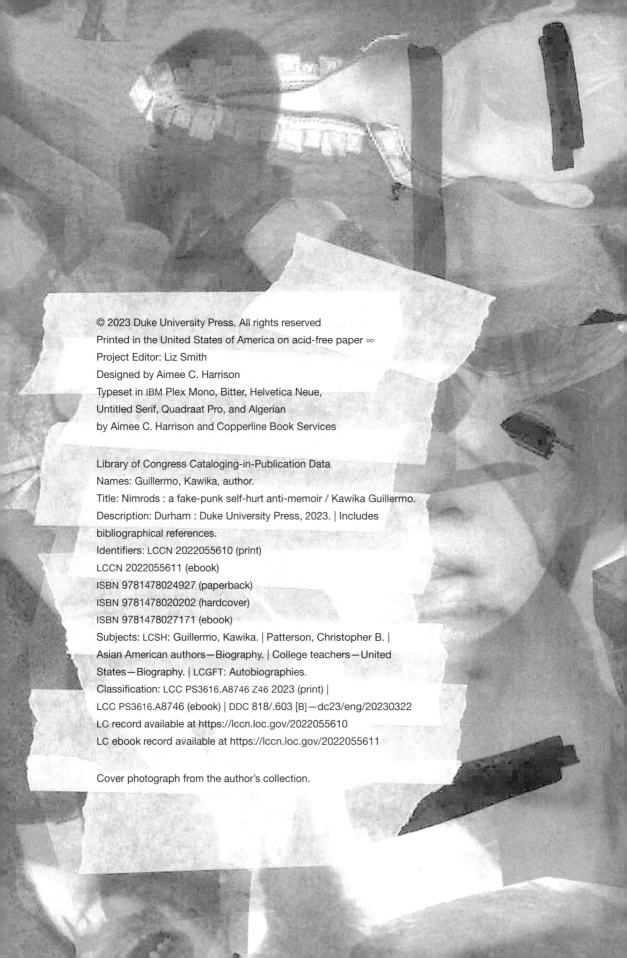

Project Editor: Liz Smith
Designed by Aimee C. Harrison
Typeset in IBM Plex Mono, Bitter, Helvetica Neue,
Untitled Serif, Quadraat Pro, and Algerian
by Aimee C. Harrison and Copperline Book Services

Library of Congress Cataloging-in-Publication Data
Names: Guillermo, Kawika, author.
Title: Nimrods : a fake-punk self-hurt anti-memoir / Kawika Guillermo.
Description: Durham : Duke University Press, 2023. | Includes
bibliographical references.
Identifiers: LCCN 2022055610 (print)
LCCN 2022055611 (ebook)
ISBN 9781478024927 (paperback)
ISBN 9781478020202 (hardcover)
ISBN 9781478027171 (ebook)
Subjects: LCSH: Guillermo, Kawika. | Patterson, Christopher B. |
Asian American authors—Biography. | College teachers—United
States—Biography. | LCGFT: Autobiographies.
Classification: LCC PS3616.A8746 Z46 2023 (print) |
LCC PS3616.A8746 (ebook) | DDC 818/.603 [B]—dc23/eng/20230322
LC record available at https://lccn.loc.gov/2022055610
LC ebook record available at https://lccn.loc.gov/2022055611

Cover photograph from the author's collection.

in loving memory of
Y-Dang Troeung
1980 - 2022

you were my spirit
my ocean
my brick of a fist

once more
let us stroll
another shore

pray
to the seas
please

NIMRODS

IN VOCATION

can't write for shit these days (fatherhood & covid et al.)

this book began under the smothering covers of journal sheets

this book began when my brother and I asked each other if we missed
our father and we both said the same word

this book began in 2016 when my father voted for the future president

this book began in 2017 when my son was born & I promised he would
never meet his grandfather

this book began in early 2019 when I believed my father's death was
a blink away & he'd never be around to read it

this book began huddled in quarantine; my father in a factory

this book began in the preoccupations of the professorial confession

this book began before I was born

this book began & began & will begin again

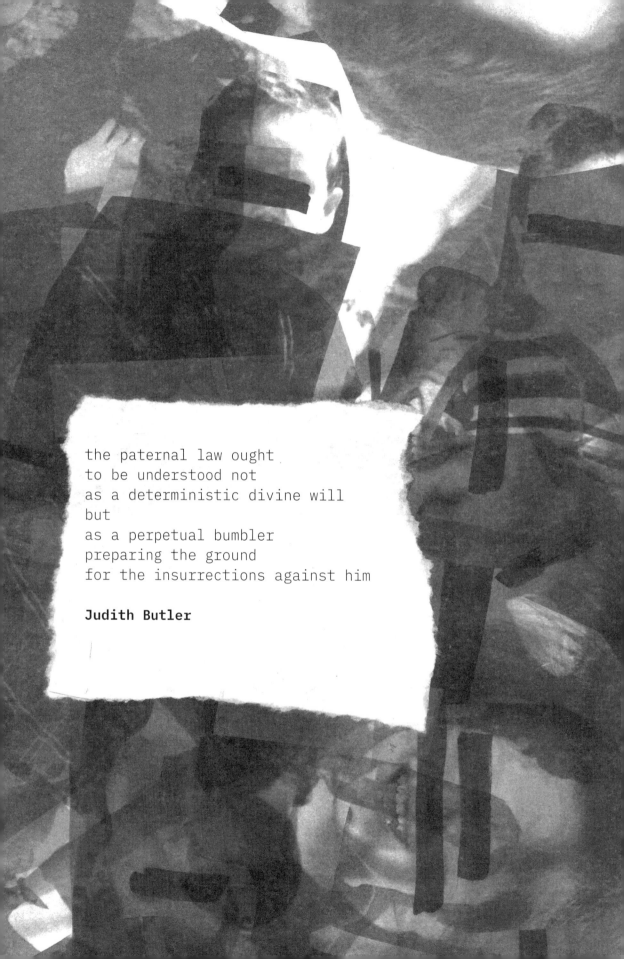

the paternal law ought
to be understood not
as a deterministic divine will
but
as a perpetual bumbler
preparing the ground
for the insurrections against him

Judith Butler

strophe

ode to patriarchy

NICE GUYS READ THIS LAST

I wake to my son
        bleating
more goat
        than child

atoms materialize in my
        breath and ribs
the calf's ear
        piercing whine

I catch my
        self thinking
I can't do
        this anymore

when will it end?
        it being
fatherhood. My son
        bleats

I wake

when I learned I was going to be a father I was in hanoi quaffing bia hơi
while perched atop a red plastic stool

                                                                    my

first thought was that an early reckless death was now forever off the table

                                                                    I

began to hope for a girl

                                                                    be

cause my child is a boy he is more likely to take after his father and take
and take but never take an affirmative step to deal with his own shit like
being the mixed-race straight-presenting white-passing all-perpetrating
son of an eye-rolling

                                                                    wmaf

someone else's baggage will be forever heavier than

                                                                    my

son who will come from a long line of men who die drunk and grasping at
reflections of the throbbing high

                                                                    moon

I lift my son. I consider saying

I LOVE YOU then

how meaningless is

I LOVE YOU he

would say

I LOVE YOU in

cessantly while tossing toys

I LOVE YOU how

I came to fear the phrase

I LOVE YOU its

intensity its expectations its constant being

I LOVE YOU keeps

you holds you would do anything any thing to save you

I LOVE YOU and

I want to shove that pacifier up your nose

Not even a real minority. Not really even marginalized. Marks of sin, trespass. Sooner or later.

       but does he even count
       as a diversity hire

       and does his inner child
       still cluster

How does it feel to be ~~a~~ problem***atic***?

            u r
           / |
hapa, traitor, bi, — ~~blacklisted~~

       ~~the~~ success ~~of~~ my
       ~~suc~~cess ~~story~~

       ~~tol~~erate my
       ~~am~~bi~~guous~~ bod~~y~~

       anal~~yze~~ my
       cauc~~asian roots~~

       bear ~~witness to my~~
       back~~ground~~

x
x
x
x
x
x

In case you didn't know, I am a professor in an Institute for Social Justice. I make money teaching kids to hate their parents.

During my first class, I ask students to write their family histories and explore the ways that power and resource-grabbing has permitted them to attend this university.

I do not join them. I walk the room, check my phone, try to memorize their names, mull over the library gardens, eye the clocktower monument to the pioneers, and glance at an oak bench upon which a committee has paid someone to carve the statements of refugees.

```
"The most surprising thing about coming to Canada was
 to see a person walking ahead of me and holding open a
 door until I could put my hand on it. Where I come from
 people were taught to kill..."
        —W——, Rwanda

"...when I moved to Vancouver, I thought that home
 was a safe place, a place of prosperity. But now I
 understand that home is home because of identity..."
        —M——, South Sudan

"...whenever I start to complain about university work,
 I think of my father and how he had to leave in the
 middle of his degree because someone decided to start a
 war..."
        —T——, Croatia

"...while so many others came from such difficult
 circumstances, I had nothing to run from, nothing to
 escape."
        —Chris, Canada
```

the academy has taught me to isolate the past into weapons of my
own making

arc

hive text stories of my family's migration from ilocos norte to hawaii
their offspring's fornications with indigenous japanese korean
cambodian black and haole people

re

silence in the face of war poverty and white supremacy carve the
past into weapons I keep in a box to pull from whenever I need a
past of seeds caught in trade winds but there is another past not
of seeds coming to root but of ships coming to settle the past of
my white grandfather who preached from a pulpit that divorce
and homosexuality were certain routes to hell the past of my uncle
who retreated from his father's insanity and died in los angeles of
hiv-related illness

no

one in the family talked about him and if asked they would get
choked up or pretend to sometimes the past is not an archive
it's the white uncle a

ski

ng you at your own grandmother's funeral how you learned to
speak english

an o   de of
debts o wed
to   myself

if a brown man falls
in a forest of white ever
greens does anyone
feel appalled?

to whom do I owe
the power behind my voice
what strength I have become?

hide your heart until it
grumbles like a thunder
that pounds your body
into the storm

armor lurks below death's door

we work the floor

wake work: the work of dwelling in the wake of

> *plotting, mapping, and collecting the archives of the everyday*
> *of Black immanent and imminent death*

ode work: the work of giving honor and respect in a way that also
dismantles that honor

I do not know how to speak of the dead without the song of odes

I cannot speak of elders without counting the owed

I cannot reach the paths without anodes

> without working to

strip out

every piece

of rusted ore

x
x
x
x
x
x

my son will live in the owed ac

counting for un
counted broken treaties &
counted plantation sakadas from ilocos who
counted the sugar that fed the
counted migrants of the dust-bowl plains rescued by the un
counted airplanes that
counted 7.6 million tons of explosives dropped not
counting the un
counted genocide & its unac
counted aftermath where un
counted reliance on all the isms that will guide him to
count whether or not he is a man whether he
counts in the way others
count

someone said each kid
eliminates one book

what did I sacrifice for you?
what did you write for me?

what can storms build
out of the trees they fall?

how much slack can
we give to what writhes
at the line's end?

can new grammar
overcome the violence
of abstraction?

there is a lot
to mourn to warm to
warn

and work
to be done

x
x
x
x
x

GET IN THE CAR

Middle school, I get in the car with my father. The scent of something I don't know what it is, but I smell it whenever something bad happens. My father turns off the headlights as he bullets down a hill toward my grandparents' house, singing *she's got a ticket to ri-ide* as Douglas firs toss by like spears.

High school, I'm visiting home from Las Vegas. My father turns off the headlights on a long stretch of road so we can see the moon. A smell floats upon the stagnant air and he lowers his window to get rid of it, singing *pleased to meet you hope you guess my name*. The firs ask me why I got in the car; my arms dig into the seat; I can't breathe.

Graduate school, I'm visiting home from Seattle. I get in the car. My girlfriend is here to meet my father. He controls the steering wheel with only his knees, singing *some people claim that there's a woman to blame*. He grills us on our politics, accuses her of being a feminist. The headlights are off; she grips my hand; the firs gasp.

Junior professor, I'm visiting home from Nanjing. My father opens the passenger side door. That scent again, like the needles of the firs. He sings *momma loves her ba-by* and turns off the headlights so we can see the stars.

My father is a big bald white man who wears plaid shirts, light
blue jeans & trucker hats. & yes we were all afraid of him.
Most everyone was & if they weren't yet it was only a matter
of time.

even when he was home, he was out
                on another drunken sabbatical

no waking him from this stupor, my mind
                two thousand light years away

M   e   a   ba d   man who   laid sh   i   t
b   e   ans &   r ats & yes we   re all afraid of
M   e   &   yet it   s only
      me

even   out

                  his   t   or   y

16

x
x
x
x
x
x

mori-bound intermittent
    swatting at the wall, each slap
        with considerably less gusto

maso-chismo psychotic
    fitfully drunk in bed, flying sweat
        enchanted by dirt-marked threads

tight-lipped ironic
    morning habit when he arranges omelets, sloppily
        into a funny face

I never say it aloud.

My dad was an alcoholic

It seems unfair to say that about someone who loved me so much.

But yeah he would throw shit and scream and call women whores and do pretty unhinged shit sometimes and usually liquor was mixed in there and yeah he also lost his marriage and his kids and multiple jobs and the respect of everyone and yeah to this day he still gets drunk and binges and screams and acts out because he can't fucking stop himself.

I never say it alou

My dad was an alco

   see   so   lo

Bu yea he wou thro   an scre   and all women who   an
    pretty   shit so
there an   yeah
                                to this day he
                                   can fuc   stop

I never say

My dad was

Grandma and Grandpa loved their youngest child, my father, their Baby.
Unlike their other children, Baby wasn't gay, or broken by war, or adopted,
or mentally ill, or anorexic, or a woman. Baby's big eyes made even the
gray skies look Blue.

`Your dad is so great.`

And Drunken Fits? Baby Blue was full of those.

Baby Blue liked his booze, he liked to hide it around the house, inside the
toilet tank, like where you might hide a gun before an executive decision.

`I feel so bad for your dad.`

I hate to say it because mentioning it always made it worse. One day
he may decide to switch the bottle for the gun. And we pitied him more
than we did ourselves.

`Are you gonna include the time he left y'all at`
`the five-cent arcade place for hours because he`
`went and got drunk and forgot about you? And you`
`called me to come pick you up!`

But, Sis, the least he could do, before going on a bender, was leave us
at the arcade.

All aboard!

Malcolm loved Elijah. His rail was not one of those bullshit BETA CUCK sit-ins.

Let's get in the car! STAND UP AND FIGHT LIKE A MAN said Malcolm to Jimmy

Martin too, so intensely, inescapably MACHO; if it wasn't their route to ALPHAdom it had to be our own.

God Daddy, Jesus Daddy, Marx Daddy, Freud Daddy, Darwin Daddy, lez-go, lesbos!

My colleague teaches a course on women, and all her assigned texts are written by Daddy Shakespeare.

Lezgo, Poundy Daddy, Joycy Daddy, Faulky Daddy, Hemmy Daddy!

I was brought to literature because a blonde girl I liked loved Charles Dickens. She loved books almost as much as she loved Rush Limbaugh. She called the other girls feminazis.

I followed her to community college English classes and when I realized they were seventy percent women reading books that glorified male desire I was forever in the carnal caboose.

The last I talked to her she was getting her PhD at Columbia, copiously quoting white French men, disappointed that I hadn't yet read Lyotard.

Baby Blue chose to skate on the thin mud ice of miscegenation.

What did he believe would happen when he decided to bring home a little lady from the islands, whose luggage included a six-year-old Black daughter? How did he expect his friends and family would react when he fathered a pair of brown twin sons?

    I wish I had your father.

Baby Blue claims he comes from the cool, cool plains. A beer or two later and he's back in that loco motive, wondering why some people are allowed to switch compartments, why some get free tickets to second class, and who *who* was watching over the line?

    Your dad is so kind and nice.

I blame my father for lots of my shit. I wish I had the wisdom of the past tense, to say "I once blamed my father."

    Your father is so good looking.

Well, in the end, Baby Blue married not one, but two Filipinas. So how about them apples? Or is it mangoes? Either way, go suck 'em.

baby blue believes he is descended from an apache princess

some have said that apaches didn't have princesses

baby blue believes he is descended from irish

some have said that the irish were the black people of europe

baby blue believes he is distanced from the grave crimes

perhaps he meant to save both his family and my mother's

we share stories of immigration, oppression, colonization

we share beliefs in claims and titles

we share cascade bridges

we share the discipline of the masculine

we share poached flesh

caught from the waves and released

into the speechless stream

The stars of Asian America ain't Daddys. They're Grace Lee Boggs, Maxine Hong Kingston, Jessica Hagedorn, Lisa Lowe. More women writing about Asian America than men, more women writers than men, and something's still wrong with Frank Chin.

all ye Asian American daddies

The first Asian American novel I ever read was Kingston's *The Woman Warrior*. I felt called upon. Somehow, a Chinese American woman author spoke to me more intimately, more truthfully, than my family, my friends, my God.

of the real and the fake

I came to learn, as every Asian American scholar does, that *The Woman Warrior* is a controversial text. In the 1980s and 1990s, it was the most popular novel taught on college campuses. In the years that followed, the book received so much pushback, so much whining and feet-dragging and knuckle-mashing and dick-measuring by undone Asian men, that Kingston's next two books were entirely about men. Her fourth book, perhaps a change in direction, got incinerated in a house fire.

get in the car

The warrior writer of Asian America, my intimate caller, spent her career seeking peace from the alpha dragons.

I never think of myself as smart. In my own head I'm an idiot—a slow, fat, brown impostor.

I wish for the past tense, to say, "I used to never be able to think of myself as smart."

Why are you so mean to your father?

Baby Blue's son once won the school reading competition. A mere fourth grader, the boy claimed to have read over a thousand pages in a week! An obvious lie—how could this child, brown, slow, obsessed with video games, have beaten the high schoolers at reading?

We all know monkeys can't read.

Baby Blue knew this to be true. Baby Blue dubbed his son a liar.

Baby Blue offered his own wisdom.

Sometimes we lie to ourselves so much we believe it's true.

Baby Blue was disappointed in his lying son and the boy's bullshit tear-stained eyes.

OMG I'M TURNING WHITE LIKE MY DAD

When my family moves from Hong Kong to Vancouver in 2018, I'm the American yokel, the arrogant overpublished chauvinist who stands tall while the smoke around him clears.

The next year, I'm counting numbers with my son, when an image on Facebook pricks my sight: the Prime Minister of Canada, Justin Trudeau, in a full-body-paint Aladdin costume, his arms over angular white women as if pretending to abduct them. The headline says he wore brownface at a 2001 gala when he was a teacher at the West Point Grey Academy in Vancouver.

I look up the school. It's two miles from our apartment.

Over the next week, I learn a lot about my colleagues and my new city. They are disappointed, but not angry. They are worried about how this will all go down on the news. But nobody asks me, as the father in a brown family, how this is going down for me.

Few people think that one incident in brownface (which escalates to two more in blackface) is a reason to withhold a vote. Few people think that October 2001, one month after 9/11, when violence against Muslims and anyone Muslim-looking had skyrocketed 1,700 percent and the US was in-discriminately bombing Afghanistan to hell, was a bad time to walk the streets of a multicultural city in a costume that said *your face is my punchline*.

quick to coat
the unprimed minister
their moment in the movement
to join the black
faced parades

too brown
to frown
wait 'til they get you
in an arabian
gown

the reluctant fly
in the fumed ointment
that treats
the brown residues
of a diaper rash

this where my son will live with
these people these people these people
who insist to hug you
so their faces never need look you
in the eyes

we
planets of galaxy diversitas

       some larger than others
       some darker than others
       some in strange ellipticals
       some with icy crowns
       some nearer to the void
       some so small and far away
       some no longer count as planets

we
each our own gravitas

       romanized mythological
       circling solar
       depth where
       creation pulls

all the toms
in new age gowns

       my father
       haole a-hole
       the elliptical that draws
       our gravity

but can
a planet please stop circling the sun?

I once saw myself in Aladdin, even though he was a different kind of
brown and his face was modeled off Tom Cruise.

Quick, cunning, nipple-less chest, Aladdin taught
        me that when

they say "Asian people," complimentarily, they never mean
        me and when

they say white people, disparagingly, they do mean
        me and when

they say us, they mean
        me only insofar as I pass

their tests and when they say
        them that is one of

their tests. And this: my dear Fil-Am
        me they will still give

their children the surnames of
        their fathers and

their brown faced photographs are still just one step away
        from exposure

from where, my son will ask, does our brownness come? And I will
declare
        a hole

a colleague's family visit

While playing with our son, their four-year-old daughter says, casually, "brown is disgusting." Not brown like chocolate, but brown like skin. Dis

cuss

ting. The parents' faces are red with embarrassment. My wife and I try to laugh it off. We ask, as if to puncture the wound again, "our baby is brown—do you think he is dis

gusts

ting?" We do not know it, but we are testing them: the parents as well as the child. The girl just keeps gaz

sting

at our son. But we are battle ready with recoded verge for it makes no difference whatever utterance she makes.

Ten things to tell my father:

#1:   you voted for Trump twice and trampled anyone on
        social media who disagreed
            and you are white

#2:   you married a Filipina you never bothered to learn
        was Ilocana
            and you are white

#3:   you suffered from alcoholism, depression, suicidal
        ideation
            and you are white

#4:   you worked far harder, for far longer, for far less pay
        than I ever will
            and you are white

#5:   a Korean woman once worshipped you, believing you
        were God (she told me this when you got up to use the
        john)
            and you are white

O asian men
we CUCKS of America
we BETABUXXED of BUXXOM lovers
we CHANGS to their CHADS

we CURRY CELIBATE
take our FEMOIDS
we'll be snorting
BLUEPILL powder beside

other wallflower pornamentation
LAY DOWN, rot
get your EZ NUT
of RICEPILL swallowers

our LOOKSMATCH so why not
let me ROAST
be the MOG
upon the ROPE

we word smiths
with imagery entice
and straddle dazzle
the qua train

four things only mixed brown kids know:
1) as a child, everyone says we're beautiful because no one knows our kind of ugly
2) as a teenager, no one acknowledges we exist, so we throw donuts at passing cars to see what racial epithet people will scream at us
3) I see it now, you're actually white Mexican Black Indigenous
4) no lanes just the intersection of down and brown

I've told many people, casually, that I hate my last name, "Patterson"
1) I chose to write fiction under a different name, my mother's name
2) my wife did not take my father's name, and neither did my son
3) my sister changed her last name back to my mother's
4) my brother moved an ocean away and never returned

when a father divorces
1) wife gone, kids gone
2) no one around to hurt
3) no one who needs him
4) to stay sober

x
x
x
x
x
x

#6:   you were a janitor, a gas station attendant, a caretaker for
        the mentally disabled, a middle school teacher, an Amazon
        contract worker
                and you are white

#7:   I was a janitor once
                a warehouse worker, a middle school teacher

#8:   I nearly had your life
                I would not have survived

#9:   perhaps I
                did not

#10:   perhaps you
                did not

MIXED being white

MONGREL whassup

HALFIE playing around like

HAPA and ma who stole it from kanaka maoli but

HALFU still not getting it?

MUTT nowhere is home and anyway

SHIT ain't anyone in this city ever seen some real

TRASH before? The kind that streaks across paper and it could be a

TURD or leftover chocolate? What else would you call

DIRT like us? The father who had no dreams but they were stolen anyway.
The mother who takes what she wants when she doesn't want it anyway.
The son who didn't ask his family's permission to write this book but did it
anyway. Neither we they nor

FUNGUS likes to be contained, nor to think of themselves as containable. Like the
father who claimed he was the first person to call someone a

NIMROD and why not it's
A-HOLE
BROWN
WORLD

x
x
x
x
x

REPUGNANT

My parent's wedding: my mother, barely tall enough to shove
a VHS into the movie slots at Blockbuster, next to my father, head
above the sugarcane fields where his new father-in-law was born.

"Your father must be white?"

their

fucking

on

my

skin

"Is that really your son?"

our kind of skinship:

his radiance

reigns the radical of

her roots

a boy's melody to hell

the gateways coming clean for the first time
the impetus self-damning dark-plumaged dove
the onanistic desires of mangled guts pretending
the nude sodomites of twenty-three with ADD
the rape culture tongues of boom headshot
the pulpy desires penetrating secret societies
the ode-writing lovers breeding glowworms
the angel fire scraping away dark edges
the assumed absolutions of chaotic butterflies
the magnetic ecstasy of Foley in drag
the devil whose lips hold a million secrets
the stunning solemnity of building-burning pressure
the self-flagellating papacy of love with restraints
the postulant order of alarm-setting charms
the ecumenical tribes learning to eat bread again
the homoerotic homophones of the bye boi bi boys
the brutal hymns of rough surf on the coast
the gospel of his big western arms
the commandments of the coarsest, commonest pleasures
the anti-synoptic miracles of turning music into mud

x
x
x x
x x
x x
x

I grew up in a working-class neighborhood in Portland, Oregon, the whitest
big city in the United States.

                                        when I was twelve, my uncle died

My parents were both preachers' kids who met on the evangelical routes
between Hawaiʻi and Oregon.

                                            I was kept from his funeral

I was the only non-white person in my class besides my twin brother.

                                    I heard whispers—"gay," "HIV," "AIDS"

Manhood was a game I could never win.

                                        his words dripped like dinuguan

In time I grew so far from this thing, "man."

                                        I did not know lips could lisp

I began to see beauty in the blurred-off distance.

                                            that lips could be eternal

I grew up dreaming of androgynous punk rock stars with inky black hair.

Karen O, Korean-born yelper spitting on herself onstage.

Billie Joe, pink punk rebel, hot mess, Chaplin Tramp, baiting bicon, slurring every word with a nimble tongue,

      guitar

          strapped

               so low

                    his strums

                    punched

I had a hard time believing that anyone could look at that man, whose body language invited desire, who sang in contradictions and nonsense, and not feel bashed.

My sexuality became a faith-based conviction,

      dear god,

         I can't be

             the only one here

                 solidly breathing in

                    this wondrous

                    air

I was twenty-two, sitting at a bear bar in Seattle, when I first opened up about my bisexuality. I was surrounded by friends; lucky for me, because it didn't take long for some white biker to overhear our conversation and spike my drink with two drops of mystery liquid. My friend A___ wrestled him to the ground while I ordered another drink, wearing a smile to hide my quivering lips.

I spent the next decade slipping into clubs, gay and not-so-gay, dancing, kissing, and sometimes getting pressed into corners by large white men who looked at me and saw a smooth Asian bottom.

I spent a year in Asia. Then, I spent five years traveling to Asia every summer. Then, I lived in Asia for five years.

in Asia I
could get away
from just
being Asian

Ten statistics my son will need to know:

1) As a man, you'll be three and a half times more likely to commit suicide than a woman. You'll be six times more likely to be killed by someone with a gun, and over ten times more likely to be incarcerated.

2) If you are bisexual, like your father, you'll be twice as likely to be depressed as a straight person, and nearly twice as likely to commit suicide as a gay or lesbian person. You'll have a far higher chance of drug and alcohol abuse, and of being a victim of sexual abuse.

3) As an Asian North American, you will be three times less likely than a white person to seek mental health treatment, and far less likely to report sexual assault.

4) As the mixed-race child of two mixed-race parents, you'll be an alloy with few allies, a compound in a world of natural elements.

5) You might convince yourself that everyone is wearing a face, holding their breath, waiting for you to rust.

At

                  thirteen

 my

       parents   divorced

 and

         my   mother   moved

 my   brother

          and   me   to

 Las   Vegas   a   land   of

        tough   talking   Latin

  os and Filipino fathers   running   every   barbecue
I returned to this orbit, manhood. I lost my virginity. I learned to talk
tough I   read   *The*   *Game* and   believed   that the

same   strategies   I   used   to   win   video

  games   could be   trans

  ferred   to win

        ning   women
   I   went   to   a
  megachurch and listened to the preacher say
"it is the duty of all women to be cheerleaders for their husbands." The
  next day I told this to my girlfriend and

she   slapped me so hard my head

  never   stopped

         spinning

In my twenties I began to lose weight. I went from two hundred pounds to one-fifty, on a diet of quiet anorexia, believing that losing weight would make my body more feminine and easier to hide.

> how small and narrow the boxes are
> for little boys

I had a child before I could finish. In the hospital I thought only of my partner. My child, another boy, a future man, was causing her pain. He was the reason our research had stalled. He was the reason we had to move from dynamic Hong Kong to damp, amicable Vancouver.

> and at some point you internalize the box
> and it becomes your home

Getting angry at the future-man, smashing his pacifier, tossing him up to PLAY.

> patriarchy: its beats, its lines, its rhymes, its belting hymns, its catchy
> hooks

6) As a Filipino, you'll have a ninety percent chance of living your life plagued by the question generations of men could not answer: "What is a Filipino?"

7) As someone born in Hong Kong, you will meet people who will never be satisfied until they dig this information out of you.

8) As the great-grandson of a family of preachers, born-agains, and true believers, you'll be taught to obey, to believe in myth, perhaps, even to think of white Americans as morally superior. Your father will try to protect you from this. But belief will offer you manhood.

9) As the son of a refugee . . .

10) As the . . .

(There is information crucial for your survival in this world and I don't know it.)

When I was nineteen I started calling myself atheist.

that must be, like, super fucking hard for you

Rather than explain why, I avoided my parents and didn't bring it up to anyone.

like, that must be super fucking hard for you

A year later, I broke up with my girlfriend of four years.

that must be super, like, fucking hard for you

Rather than explain why, I moved to Seattle alone, with no savings.

that, like, must be super fucking hard for you

They say that bisexuals are privileged because we do not need to come out.

that must be super fucking hard, like, for you

Because we can pass as straight.

that must be super fucking hard for, like, you

At times, I admit, it has been a privilege to hide.

Gorg! I am twistin up the chaps, cuz you are, like, dry ass fuck!

SCAT

When the Patterson family moved to Portland from Texas and Tennessee, they were the yokel Bible-thumpers from the cotton fields armed with shotguns and a southern drawl. It was the 1970s, and the South was measured in dog attacks and redneck sheriffs with rolls of fat on their necks. And my grandfather was the spitting image of white tyranny.

> Dr. W___ Patterson Jr., 1921–2014: Born in a Texas farmhouse. Learned to fly. Fought for the navy in World War II. Earned a PhD in religiosity. Became a pastor. Planted a church in Pearl Harbor. Became dean of a Christian school in Portland, where his son and grandson would one day enroll. Wrote thirteen how-to books about the Gospel, with titles like *Search for True Discipleship*.

my life if anything is an attempt to destroy the legacy (even if no one ever reads my work, even if I die in obscurity, fuckers, I'm taking you with me)

My elder uncle faced hell. Adopted out of New Orleans at the angry age of twelve, he was the only Patterson son old enough to fight in Vietnam. He came back with wobbly knees, PTSD, and spats of Agent Orange that would forever lurk in his system. It was difficult for him to be around me, my father once told me, because I looked like the enemy.

R__ Patterson (??–Present): Disabled. Diabetic. Likes to joke around.

my life if anything is an attempt to deal with the could-have-beens (in hell, all are heroes)

> my sister's father was a mixture of black, white,
> and kānaka maoli, and none of us siblings ever
> met him

In 2011, on a Christmas visit to my white family, I noticed there
was not a single nonwhite person in the church audience. Someone
in the pews stared at me, disapprovingly. Later, he asked my
cousin, "Who the heck was that Black guy sitting in our church?" I
guess I had a shaved head.

> my sister got the worst of the bush-fire stares
> at fifteen, when she came to church trying to hide her
> pregnant belly with a black hoodie
> she got smoked right out

In 2015, on another Christmas visit, I went for a midday jog around
my grandparents' suburban hillside. When I returned, a police
car was leaving the house. A neighbor had called the cops after
spotting a suspicious Black man breaking out of my grandparents'
house, wearing running shorts and Nikes. Thankfully, nothing had
been stolen. I guess I was wearing a hoodie.

> my sister changed her last name and
> moved herself and her son to the afflicted desert
> she blacked them all out

I still visit my white family. I eat their food and take their money
for my birthday.

My aunt had issues. They all did, of course, but because she was the only daughter, she did not have growing pains, or make mistakes. She had issues.

P___ Patterson (1957–Present): A registered nurse and caretaker for her father and mother in their last days. Wife and mother twice over. Moved in with her parents when their health began to fail. Has the issues.

my life if anything is an attempt to doubt the disease (cracker, dogeater, island hopper, heathen mulatto)

Metro Christian Church, 2019: At the Chinese buffet after my grand-mother's funeral, my great-uncle feels the need to stop everything and ask what I'm doing there. And how—he demands—did I ever learn to speak English?

I am
paranoid
and
surrounded
by
evidence

Over time, I've learned to transform

atheist

proteus

of

the

shifting

seas

a   thetis   toward   the

family

craft

Adopted out of a hospital in Dallas, my younger uncle, Danny, was a magician. He fooled his parents into believing he liked women. He tricked his family into believing he was happy and healthy after he moved to LA. He seduced me into loving him when I wasn't supposed to idolize the damned. His vanishing trick left us waiting.

Daniel Durwood Patterson (1956–1996): [No record exists.]

my life if anything is an attempt to lure back the ghosts (come back from your magic trick, uncle danny, come back)

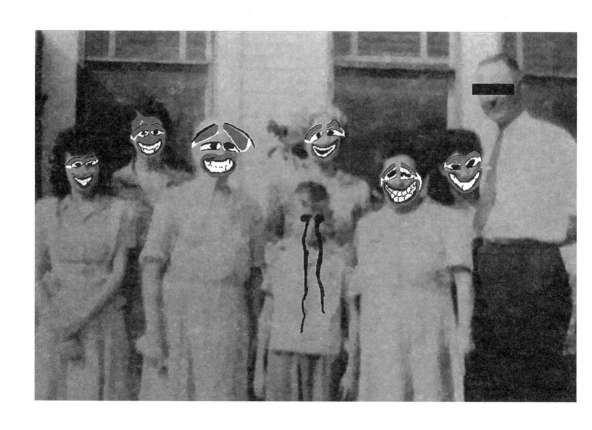

DOING TIME

After his brother died, my father lost it.

At first *it* was every job he could get until he became the sole janitor at my nonaccredited Christian middle school; the same school where his father had become dean; the same school where his mother had worked for over a decade teaching science classes.

Every day after school, my brother and I would help my father carry out the trash. During classes, we kept black garbage bags in our pockets to replace the hallway canisters so they did not overfill. When the other students found out, they started to leave trash on the floor and bubble gum under the desks, knowing we would have to clean it up. I felt ashamed, but I can't imagine the shame of watching your darker-skinned twin sons clean up after the white bullies.

In 1999, *it* was my mother. "Escaped," "fled," "rescued us" are all words I've used to describe what happened. The last straw, as my mother tells it, was when he drove us to Grandma's house, drunk.

In time, I did not blame myself for *it*; I reveled in my father's distance. To be away from him was to lose the screaming fits, the broken dishes, the daily church visits, the eyes of a moral overseer, the face of a ticking watchman all wounded up.

it all began with NIMROD
rebel against god
and scale the towering babel

he carries with him
a fishing rod and worms
his favorite lure

did you try to save
yourself? an aa
meeting, getting help?

I'd rather be

Lucifer

than just another

Isaac

this is what
makes the idea
of including religion
in politics and
faith-based activism so
inconceivable
for me

you ask for proof

we give you truth

you find new friends

to believe your myths

Away from my father in Las Vegas, everything became a game, especially raising hell. I found a group of golden boys, all of us from broken families. When I remember my teenage years, I don't recall proms or recitals. I remember bruises, sores, slaps, sirens, & how

at home we
prank called
old women's houses &
on halloween we
tossed pumpkins against
garage doors &
at cornerstone park we
broke the sprinkler
system so that
on blocks of ice we
could slide
down hills &
at sunset mall we
shouted at the fathers
across the gaps that
one day we
would sleep with
their daughters &
at eldorado casino we
snuck into the buffet &
ate our fill &
at heritage park we
chugged milk gallons to
see who vomited first &

at wal-mart we
got 86'ed for playing chicken
with shopping carts &
at another wal-mart we
pretended to be
disabled so
in wheelchairs we
could play
chicken again &
on boulder highway we hurled
donuts & used condoms at
passing cars &
at wendy's we
mooned unsuspecting
families &
at graduation rehearsal we
streaked naked
through a baseball field &
on the strip we
squeezed our nipples to
photo-bomb tourists &
inside circle pits we
bashed each other
in the nuts so we couldn't

it all began with NIMROD
accuser father
death dazzled drunk

left our family dog
out to die in the backyard
for the neighbor to rescue

ninth grade drop out
he learned of family only
they're there to push you out

I'd rather be

Lost

than just another

Found

now that my father was
irrecoverable
I wished that he had been
beside me so that
I could have searched his face
for the answers which
only the future would
give me now

when asked about you

we only say

sacred state

rescue

After my parents' divorce, I had no need for a male role model. The women in my family were male enough.

My mother and sister were insensitive and promiscuous baseball-bat-wielding tomboys. My sister with her lack of social tact and affection for Pearl Jam and NWA was my natural way of being a woman.

I get my ball-bats from my sister, my slap-sticks from my mother, and my insatiable lust—and need to always talk about this lust—from both.

My mother, role model for ambition, has gourmandizing desires. She never takes a break, never goes on vacation without turning in her five-hour days. I can never match her discipline, her waking at six a.m. to jog, swim, bike, or triathlon all three at once.

My sister never had a piercing but has tattoos. She wears no jewelry, and shops in the men's aisles. She insists on keeping a baseball bat in her trunk in case shit starts to go down. Once, when I asked her about her sexuality, she said she just took whatever she could get.

This runs in us, we the women of my family, and the women-minded.

This so-called masculine aspect, masculine desire, masculine aggression.

This taking whatever we can get.

one day in a white suburb we

felt the ride and our

fun end when at the golden hour we

golden boys strode down from atop the city's mesa to play with air rifles

the kind that look i

dentical to real shotguns and m16s I

snuck around my friend A___'s wealthy white

neighborhood pretending I

was a terrorist in *counter strike* keeping my

rifle tight to my chest I

opened a gate heard a whisper and crept backward I

heard the whirrrl of a helicopter and when I

looked up to see it a spotlight

hit my

eyes and a white

ness eviscerated my

sight

FREEZE DROP IT HANDS IN THE AIR

the gun fell and some

one threw me into a garage door harder than I

could throw a pumpkin I

was handcuffed flattened against the hood of a police car I

wasn't muffled but my

words just bounced off their armor until A___

emerged from the garage hands up fair skin mirroring the setting sun

and I

felt the hands on my

grips begin to

slide

A couple years after the divorce, when my father moved to Las Vegas to
be near us I thought he was weak so much weaker than my mother and
sister he had accepted a dismal salary teaching at a low-funded
elementary school in the deeply segregated area of North Vegas the
kids hated him he said because he was white he did not think this was
fair because he was poor and had to work a night job just to afford his
studio apartment away from his family and his religious   *but*
community my father was no Baby Blue was barely scraping by *will you*
barely alive complaining whining hem-hawing pissing in his *think I'm*
panties words brought me to understand the weakness of   *crazy if I say*
this man a man who covets not a real man just a lamb   *I don't think I*
shrouded in the holy lamb's wool I discovered the word   *do it very much*
pedantic and my heart stilled then the word officious   *now no it's*
fervent ressentiment equivocator a defensive   *funny I don't think*
intellectualizing the way we marshal words even   *so either I've been*
when they have ceased to open any locks I began   *listening for it too*
to read about race and my father became clear   *and well intellectual*
white man's burden white naivete white innocen*izing is a real specific*
ce then same with suicide that is what I mean is*kind of defense it has its*
suicidal ideation   *own sound to it not this*
    but   *sound so far I may even*
    this   *know a little about where*
    explained   *it's gone I'm thinking there*
    the   *were some things that*
    both   *happened in the past few years*
    of   *that I had no defenses at all to*
    us.   *deal with it was like the maginot*
    line I marshaled the formidable practiced resources of the decades
       long war of attrition I'd fought with my depressiveness and they
           were completely irrelevant instantly shattered to bits

my feminist misogynist self has a big mouth

she likes to say that she's never dated someone younger than her as if it's a political decision

she likes to say she's never dated a white woman as if value wasn't desire

she likes to think of desire as something that can be willed into a political statement like a character in a novel or the I of a memoir

she's a liar because she long ago forced herself to see white women as ugly in fear that they would do something racist to her or they would accuse her of doing something aggressive or inappropriate to them

she's a liar because she never wanted to risk her color coloring their eyes

she's a liar because there was T___, the first and last white girl she dated, who was technically older than her by a month

she's a dick because T___was killed in a car crash. the driver, a golden boy, was high on cocaine and maybe meth. he survived without a mark. he had no remorse. he felt no need to go to her funeral

she's a dick because she fled T___'s memory and rushed through college and graduated with a BA at nineteen

she's a dick because she had to get out else resolve to go unrepaired unwashed unlettered

Before I left Las Vegas I had to break with K__, my girlfriend for five years, perhaps the only reason I never went full-on INCEL PICKUP-ARTIST A-HOLE. We fought & she said she wanted to have my child & I said well if you do that then no one will ever love you again,

& at sunset theater
I learned to MAD HUSTLE
after nearly four years of
cleaning toilets & RIPPING
used condoms from theater
seats & I got so HARD making
$5.50 an hour until they
SAT on it & promoted me to
SUPERVISOR & I made $5.75
an hour & at the TRAILER
HOMES behind sam's club
we got PINNED DEEP by
police helicopter spotlights
that tracked our SEXY ASSES
home whenever we were out
PIMPIN like VILLIANS after
dark & at best buy I got these
BADASS GUNS after lifting
HARD WEIGHTS of boxed
television sets WORKing
warehouse after a white
woman complained that
I wasn't smiling enough for
THAT ASS on the sales floor &
near the circle k in K__'s

neighborHOOD we
heard BADASS DRIVE by
SHOOTings nearly every
week & we had to duck for
cover while GETTIN MAD
SKILLS on super mario BROS
& at the intersection of the
I-15 freeway & tropicana in
my HARDcore COCKroach
infested apartment I slept
on a mattress we found in
the BIG FAT DUMPster &
lacking ac in 110° weather
I LIFTED myself by hiding
in COOL libraries & at basic
high school I learned we
were the LEAST BASIC
school in north america cuz
we had THE HIGHEST rates
of TEEN pregnancy & every
now & then some SWEET
HONEYS would offer me $10
BLOWJOBS in math clASS so
they could HIT THAT Jack in
the BOX for lunch & at the co

You named me christopher christ bearer but couldn't remember why t
his name why that time mom wanted to name me kawika you weren't
having any of that your kids wouldn't be in that gobbledygook they'd
have right christian names chris now that's a fucking name like chris
t like christmas the only fucking holiday in december christopher
like columbus the man who discovered all the brown boys w   *But*
ho couldn't fucking discover nothin and while you're at it   *that leaves*
add the middle name benjamin make his name long lik   *a mess, a mess*
e my schlong and on top of that tell him he's white te   *someone else*
ll him his hair is brown his eyes are blue his skin is *would have to clean*
pale and then tell him get this there's not a fuc*up and that's not a very n*
king god but white jesus oh my god this is s   *ice thing to do to some*
o good now the piece de resistance put h   *one. So it looks like*
er in an all white church and baptize th   *I'm stuck being alive*
e   *g*

   mon   *o*

    grel   *d*

     right

      out   *d*

       of   *a*

        h   *m*

        im   *n*

         for

        cry   *i*

        ing   *t*

          out

           loud   *!*

DEAD ENDS

April 11, 2005. I wake up still drunk from the night before. I get in the car. The broken lines of road paint are white imprints. The lights of Las Vegas flash in my rearview mirror. A lighthouse toppled on its side.

I arrive in Seattle, place of chilled stares, data-entry temp gigs. Pillowy land, iceberg isolation. Beacon on myself, I crash. I give away all my possessions, sleep on a friend's couch. I hitch a ride with a trucker.

On the road from Reno to San Francisco, the driver on shrooms, I start to story, pen in hand. A character comes in a beam of blue light stabbing the sky. Another, an eerie pastel coruscating overhead.

After a month, my brother, watching me founder from afar, quits his job, and finds me. In the passenger seat of his car, I write about a man I idealized, a pickup artist "stylish as a phantom jet."

From Atlanta to New York, the furrowed pavement shifts, turns into dark, crusted iron blocks. I move past the gunk, the mesh, the hard, cranial weight. I write a story and realize I've used the word "fruitcake" to describe a man.

After five months of sleeping in bunk beds and parking lots, we arrive back in Seattle. We sleep outside, near the shore, watching the sky brighten in a sea of light for whatever craft we might build to float upon it.

Eve says that suicide is several things all decided at once

a wish not to be
an aggression against the living
a clear message

Eve, my father, and myself, we got the first two covered in spades

that last one—sending a message—never sat easy with us

Eve shied away from violence.

I sought to obscure the message with tales of wanderlust   *as far as*
—to get lost on the road, left for dead to disease or   *I can tell*
temptation or some riotous combination of   *I meant no*
the two, so that my corpse could never be   *message death*
used to moralize or debate. I would simply cease to   *had words to*
be   *deliver*

my father, I cannot say

perhaps like Eve, he loved us too much to send us that message

or like me, he would rather perish than just say

we are the lighthouse
whose one task
is to emit a signal:
I am not
your safe harbor

x
x
x
x
x
x

In 2007, my brother and I have traveled as far as Gimhae, South Korea. On a passenger ship from Incheon to Tianjin, China, watching the cranes overhead, I see my past from afar. I craft a story about a friend who liked to joke that she was a sex worker. I realize that she was only half-joking. Sex work was her work, too.

In 2008, I bus alone through the banana-pancake trail through Thailand, Laos, Vietnam, and Cambodia. On a sweat-dampened mattress, with my body numb from a disease I later discover is hepatitis A, I craft a story in my head about a friend. I realize he did not just act racist and tell racist jokes. Racist is what he was, through and through.

In 2009, I spend three months taking trains through India and photographing unchained street cattle. I craft a story about an ex, a woman who cheated on me. It's disparaging, angry, painful. I reread it, realize cheating is not all that defined her.

In 2010, I sit upon the wooden planks of a Malacca harbor. I craft a story about a friend who did not want me to float away. I realize I did not just leave, I abandoned them. And I cannot write that down.

In a Manila hostel, I craft my stories into a tall, gleaming tower.

Years pass. I reread the stories and see myself. Confused, mean, angry, posturing to be the next alpha dragon. Ready for collapse. I store the stories into my dropbox, seven clicks deep.

In 2014, I move to Nanjing. Concrete land. Iceberg isolation. I story. I story until I am no longer me. I let a different name, my mother's name, seal my fate.

my father's favorite song

is tuesday afternoon by the moody blues

a song he imagines playing at his funeral

he reminds me every time I encounter him

always surprised I remember this last wish

playing a song at his funeral

the one message I can reliably send

for my father

we, aggressions against the living

we, graves psyching each other out

our visitors squirrels, raccoons

worms and gulls

I was the last of my siblings to make a clean break.

<pre>
        O   demon
strably   id
    le   shrugs
</pre>

My sister checked out when she was nine. My father, inebriated while holding her—a time you'd want balance to be your friend—tore her rubik's cube from her hands, smashed it against the wall, stomped on it, crushed it to pieces. He'd done this to her toys before, naturally, but this cube was special. It was the last gift from our Ilocana grandma before she died, a final message to my sister to pursue her mind.

<pre>
     a   fin
   ale   a
     c   hug
</pre>

My twin brother stopped calling him "dad" when we were nineteen. I never knew why. I assume there was some incident. Could have been drunken fighting. Could have been some religious quackery. Could have been something my father said to my brother's girlfriend. Could have been

<pre>
   time   lines
     be   are
     in   finite
</pre>

I spent my twenties in flight:
japan malaysia taiwan indonesia myanmar nepal
but the dude kept catching up

locked in bitter battles:
cold war rivals fought over asian soils
glares over shoulders

that old ruse that love and trust depend on forgiveness
but cold warring has taught us: all you need is a truce
and a third party to fight your crusades

we brown stalk reverse colonialism
de–cold war: what bonds our family
is talking mad shit about white daddy

my favorite memories with my mother and sister:
happy hours sharing stories of his explosive anger
that made us survivors

craft the boundaries
stories of retreat told backward:
islands limned in spun wire

Malcolm didn't care for his white heritage, wished to high paradise it didn't exist—prayed to Allah to expunge his blood.

in a strip club he
believed it was my first time
in holy chambers

Barack could not follow Malcolm's lead. He could not sever his grandparents away to some uncharted border, not while they were still living and breathing.

in Nanjing I'm free
no one will ever visit me
no one ever did

Suyin's fame came from her forbidden love between the races. She broke from white to Asian, from Hong Kong to the People's Republic, to Nepal, to Cambodia, charting white demise.

in Taiwan we
fell apart five years died
on streets in bedsheets

Bruce was bullied for his whiteness in Hong Kong, attacked for his Chineseness in America. Racism: the formula of fearmongers. Family, the human family, his respite.

in Hong Kong I sweet
talk her to lower standards
merry province lands

The Father—sacred clown—buffoon—blockhead—failed jester
of tall-tale dad-jokes—able to foresee nothing.

> just like my dad I'm
> into asians but I win
> cuz I'm asian too

How does a white man, who has always just existed, feel
anything?

> some writers don't like to
> write when they're too
> > pissed off it up   sets the form

What does struggle mean to him?

> > I tried to tell you but
> > > all I could say

What is the soul of the corn-fed?

> > > is that I too   work better
> > > > under   a
> > > > > dead
> > > > > > line

I work in an INSTITUTE FOR SOCIAL JUSTICE
I've been published in WOMEN'S STUDIES
QUARTERLY and FEMINIST STUDIES

I've made an art of masculinizing FEMINIST RHETORIC cuz I'm too
CRITICAL for your MULTICULTURALIST IDENTITY POLITICS BETA shit too
RADICAL for your momma's weak-ass INTERSECTIONALITY too

that's what we THEORISTS mean when we say LIBERAL
when we say WHITE-ADJACENT CIS-NORMIE SPINELESS CAPITALIST SHEEPLE
we're on another level we ALPHA DRAGON RACE CRITICAL CHADS

and every day I avoid taking care of my child
take every shortcut I can
happy to leave him with nannies daycare workers
mexican models posing
as babysitters

I don't call it HYPOCRISY but
CONTRADICTIVE
REALITY

it only hits me when I wonder
what kind of person my son
will be

what hope
could grow
from   dirt
like   me?

if I can keep this one girl with m   if I can be so lucky I will never let you
or anyone in your family anywhe   near us

          di

            vision

         die

           throws

if you haven't met my wife it's b   ause I instrumentalized it

if you never meet your grandso   t's because I engineered it to be so

I want you expunged, swept un   r, no life lines for you from this craft

         down

           hatch

         take

           fall

        jump

          out

        wind

          ow

        let

         go

       flush

        down

fuck it, can't write for sh t these days, and

             i

                  wan

                       you

                            abs

                                  ract

                              ed

                         in

                      to

                    un

                chart

            ed

          bor

        ders

         I fo

         id

          you

           in

             y life

              I kara

              hop

              you

              to

              the

              fuc

              ng

              wa

              yo

              go

              da

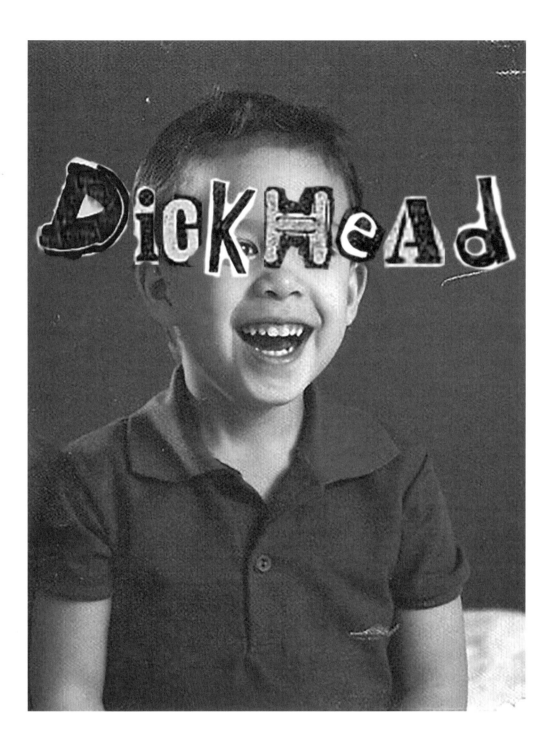

RACE POSER
FAKE
COCONUT
FATFUCK
BETRAYER
TWINKIE
WEIRD BEARD
NAME DROPPER
PRETENDER
SYNTHETIC
IMPOSTER
BANANA
APPROPRIATOR
SELF PROMOTER
A HOLE

antistrophe

holy
hai bun

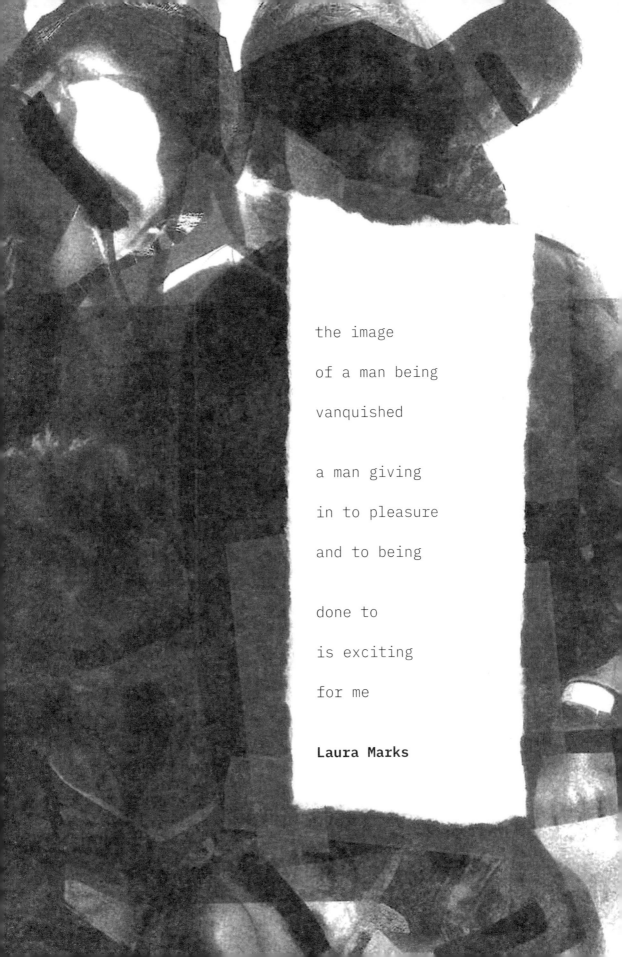

the image

of a man being

vanquished

a man giving

in to pleasure

and to being

done to

is exciting

for me

Laura Marks

SUICIDE'S LAST CALL

CHAPTER 1 VERSE 1

Wherein THE FATHER inside the bathroom of EAST COUNTY CHURCH OF CHRIST approaches the mirror[1] holding his morning coffee and sees an ugly mug and also a ceramic cup.

can't
write
for shit

these days

so;

that;

in;

Mayhaps, on June the 4th, 1994, in that in-between time after Bible Class and before Service when the mob had yet to light their tiki-torches, The FATHER stood speculating; his constitution thin, his face brown-mustached, his head balding . . .

. . . and there exiting the LORD's shitter did The FATHER see disordered bulletin board listings: African children holding Bibles; a statement on Chinese oppression of Christians; an advertisement for his FATHER's (The GRAND FATHER's) syndicate, Global English, seeking to teach the world's greatest language through the world's

---

1 On a skud skuttling round Mindoro, Butch Dalisay told me there were magical items in writing. Objects that muse in extravagant, adverb-mined prose. Shadows, windows, pictures, and most of all

mirror magic
the mage
begs us in

greatest God; a picture of The GRAND FATHER shaking hands with a man from Korea. Cofounder, teacher, perhaps...

...while thereupon, The FATHER sat in the pews of sky-blue cushion; those glossy wooden armrests, pointy, jutting out, a health hazard to the children who raced up and down the aisles after service...

...the shiny plate full of change; the splash of dullards and scents, his eyes in the copper reflection. He knew not the color of ochre; he knew not...

...but in that copper reflection, The FATHER looked there upon the first stalks of gray upon his beard; perhaps he was just a preacher's[2] son no longer...

...and yea how the copper beamed sunbeams upon The FATHER's receding hairline at the church women who found The FATHER's shiny head repellent; still, in balding The FATHER found others, older men with baseball hats, working-class FATHER archetypes hiding who they were, sharing a secret open to the public, exalted at the fact that a receding hairline correlated with higher testosterone...

wonder
zealously

could life
have been
much
different

were he born
different?

monastic

mirror

master

he has tried

to roll

with his role

_____

2 What denomination? I hear you ask. There was never a clear answer. Denominations were demonic. "Restorationist," my grandfather trained his flock to parrot.

. . . and thus for the first time in years did The FATHER sit in church alone; The Mother, The Step Daughter, The Sons, had a silent vigil of their own; boycott the boy's club out of sheer anger; trace of things to come forever; risking payment of souls for a bit of payback . . .

. . . and thus the bearded balded elder, eyes upon The FATHER's shiny temple, did saith unto him,

> how are your sons, sam?
> didn't see them in sunday school,
> and oh your daughter

they had stopped saying "step-daughter" skipping the step

and yea how The FATHER felt so trapped in his skin, his tallness, his beauty, his stature; The Preacher's son searched for truth, but his body[3] made him ignorant; truth demurred from one whose skin invited spies and lies; so he opted for the second-best enterprise: conviction . . .

. . . and henceforth did The GRAND FATHER take to the pulpit, press his glasses, and place his Bible firmly on the

---

3 I do not understand why so many would glorify a body so much like everyone else's. The white mediocre normie body: a prison of barred windows. The flock could be so kind to my father, full of smiles, but treat his Black stepdaughter with complete disdain. They would look askew at his brown sons. They would whisper about his dark wife. Everyone whispered to everyone except to him.

Black girl

pregnant and skipping service

Black girl no service

cut and dried wood where the words JESUS IS HERE were carved in a gold dust only he could see, preaching thus,

Exodus

unforgiveable

sin and then
commandme
nt four:

sundays is for
porn

Chapter Twenty Verse
Seven, Thou shalt not take the
name of the Lord thy

God in vain; for the
Lord will not hold him guiltless
that taketh his name

the unpardonable sin; this is it, boys, what we mean when we say eternal[4] . . .

. . . preacheth, I took my family to watch apollo 13; to be a Christian is kind of like that; being blown out into space; lookin' like tom hanks; Heaven, we got a problem . . .

. . . and yea how The FATHER couldn't get it together past the unpardonable sin; to misuse his name; do not worship God in a corrupt manner; that piece of halibut; a naughty bit for sure . . .

depressed in
the past

anxious in the
future, at

peace in the
present

---

4 Understand: my church was not your stereotypical cult. It was a more liberal and progressive, more penetrative and surgical type of religious brainwashing. People here knew Shakespeare, went to playhouses, spoke of their parents' civil rights activism. They were white religious hippies who refused to go to medical doctors but took echinacea pills from the local chiropractor.

x
x
x
x
x

. . . and no one mentioned The FATHER's Grand Son, son
of The Step Daughter whom they had stared out of church
at fifteen when she walked in pregnant; the faces of the
congregation; a gaggle of startled doe; pregnant black girl;
growling bear in their midst; seventeen now; lost her virginity on a dark red wool carpet . . .

bodies stand

out when
they are out

of place

. . . hence was the price of being a willful woman; a heathen coquette; child out of wedlock; cast out of God's fishing net . . .

. . . and yea The GRAND FATHER teacheth, turn to Ephesians,

> chapt' five verse twenty
> three: for the husband is the
> head of the wife as

> christ is the head of
> the church, his body, and is
> himself its savior

and thereupon The Preacher hath The FATHER thinking;
if feminists got a problem with the natural order of things,
they should pin their frustrations onto God; he's used to
it; nailed to a cross, you know . . .

. . . thus The FATHER stood alone singing monotone,
brain uttering slights, thinking, they're staring at you; you
don't deserve sainthood; lost control of your family; just

like you lost control of your brother; good for them . . .

then sings my
soul, my . . . but one day things will change . . .

sav-ior god,
to thee: how . . . the world will begin again to look more kindly on your
great type . . .

thou art, how . . . the silence you've endured is impermanent; the voice
great, thou, won't die with you; we tend to forget . . .

Art . . . not all of us marched.[5]

———————————

5 My father would never read the words of Jimmy B, that they,

    the blacks simply don't
    wish to be beaten over
    the head by the whites

But deep within the cult of love and acceptance, my father settled
for the other Jimmy B,

    some people claim that there's
    a woman to blame, but I
    know it's my own damn fault

CHAPTER 1 VERSE 2

Wherein THE FATHER recalls spending many years of his life pumping gas; he also worked at a gas station, too.

so

any

way

S/ervice ended, The FATHER took a lonesome drive home, skipping the church potluck, and remembered driving on these streets years earlier, revving his engine through the upcountry, the twin cities both named after the Bible, Damascus and Boring . . .

. . . past churches, past trailer coffee stands selling muffins and cigarettes and ionized water, past locked-up strip clubs, past diners selling trinkets of children riding fat white clouds of faux ivory . . .

keep it a little

. . . only at length, in what appeared to be a heel-dragging afterthought, did The FATHER's memory perk to that private dance turned privates massage; black girl of service; her nipples were a taste he could never recover as he tilted toward the red light till it turned into the green edges of a whirlpool . . .

sweet and simple, ease your mind

commit to speycide

. . . now at the drive thru of Fred Meyer's, The FATHER picked up a white gluey envelope that had him thinking, Ten Commandments? Nine apostles? Seven deadly sins? The trinity? All was so calculated . . .

. . . how The FATHER loved things he could not name; if only he knew the language of the body, the name of the scents, the smell of his wife's hair, the screech in her voice when they fought . . .

. . . he would never know, as if it were a sin[1] . . .

. . . what was in the medicine? He longed to know any God damn thing . . .

the plants
and herbs
and

flowers and
things that
pinched
him

cut and
stitched
him up

---

1 My father's sin was not of gluttony or sloth or pride. But he did covet things. Women's bodies, for example. Not a mortal sin, but otherwise carnal. Mostly, he coveted knowledge. He could see the way everyone looked at him, talked about him, he the preacher's son who had snuck in the only dark-skinned members of an entire congregation—us, the constant reminders that the verses they sang were to the offbeat gestures of a white man bearing a stick.

CHAPTER 1 VERSE 3

Wherein THE FATHER arrives home after a stint at his daily watering hole; and he had also visited a bar, too.

pon his home on 114th Street between Glisan and Halsey, chocka mugs proclaimed unflattering caricatures, including The Family's own mugly faces . . .

dusk the crows fly home

. . . The Mother met him with that steady gaze of unease; The FATHER's heart thudded against his chest like it had leapt onto a marble square . . .

although you weren't alive

. . . and thus the gaze hath him thinking: what the fuck[1] is gnawing her? I whipped the flock all alone; I deserved a fucking beer or three a fucking fuck fuck the things the self-righteous say when there's no dick around . . .

to see them arrive

. . . and now the reason they did not go to church; The FATHER's Second Son, Saint Christopher, still had bruises across his back; a cluster of smashed grapes from the day before, from a kid from church, a kid of baby blue eyes . . .

---

1   My father often came home drunk and tilted. I remember the lights of a van in the distance, its brights blooming into a beacon; my mother ready to scold him; us afraid she would set him off, afraid he'd toss his arm across the table and we'd all get Jimmy Buffeted away; how it would take days until we rubber duckies could bob back up to the surface.

...whereupon The Family[2] had wanted to call the parents out, to betray the flock, but this was The GRAND FATHER's flock, who flocked to his family in times of need; how could The FATHER send one to jail for battery? Toward a minor...

...and thus The Mother had truly beguilingly talked some smack; and The Step Daughter was still gone with her baby's daddy; she left before ever saying thank you for the diapers, and all because of that one tantrum or two...

wife still had to learn

...and thereupon The FATHER took a blurred glance at the photograph, at The Son's body[3]; he tried to remember where he had hidden the whiskey...

that thou who strained out a gnat

...The Sons would not catch The FATHER's face...

swallowed a camel

...the blond bully...

...son of a rich military family...

---

manholes mottled in

2 I recall my mother taking the envelope of photographs and showing me my own backside. The bruises that had stopped hurting had also been forgotten until I saw them on that glossy print. The bluish pools dotting a mud puddle would have been more visible on lighter skin.

percussive smears, neuro queer

3 "Were you injured as a child?" doctors ask me. My body speaks of ancient battles. When doctors ask these questions, I never see them again. My healthcare providers are people with limited English and the cultural injunction to give face.

upon floating isles

. . . icons of the church could not be . . .

. . . charged[4] . . .

with

no mirror
to see

me

I leaned up
to face

you

who
verses

us

in every
line

we

break

---

4 As I write this, I remember this moment clearer: my parents
taking pictures of my bruised body; the bully who beat me with a
chair leg; the welts all over my back and shoulders; the neck and
back pain I still feel to this day.

My mother said I should have hit back. I should have clubbed the
bully or outsmarted him in some way. My father told me to turn the
other cheek.

A good son always listens.

THE LAST RIDE

CHAPTER 2 VERSE 1

Wherein at THE GRAND PARENT'S house in GRESHAM, OREGON, THE UNCLE hath a wake to commemorate his long, long sleep.

what's parishable

is also perishable

uncle danny said

upon

his death

bed

T he FATHER liked feeling lost in the nonsense of the past, dizzy in the memories of his brother,[1] orbiting a dead man's gravity . . .

. . . thereupon The FATHER avoided the morbid procession by hammering at a dresser in the basement, nailing its backboard into the wall to protect his infant nephew, also named dan . . .

flatten every nail

secure every board

fabricate the home

. . . the hammer laid claim to this house where he and his brother once crawled over each other; it hadn't been that long, in the six thousand years since the universe was created . . .

---

1 Daniel Durwood Patterson died in March 1996, in Los Angeles, from HIV-related illness. I did not go to his funeral. I, queer child of ten, was not meant to mourn for the queer adult of plenty.

. . . and whilst The FATHER knew he had no right to claim this land, he felt that right anyway, cuz, you know, who the fuck was going to tell him otherwise . . .

. . . thusly The Aunt, Saint Prisca,[2] approached in slinky creaks on the stairs, wood groaning as she leaned from the steps saying, Sam, could you please lead us in prayer? . . .

. . . behold The FATHER's smile bleeding from his face as he cruised up the stairs . . .

. . . not realizing he had smuggled a ready-at-hand hammer that swayed back and forth on the radial crease of his palm . . .

. . . and came to that sacred hallway where he first kissed The Mother Saint Dion,[3] the patron saint of dying horribly, suffering needlessly, with twenty-three others . . .

. . . and all we have is names . . .

he swore
he smelled
musk

since the
beginning
of time

basements
induct
earths

voices in
chorus

heavenly
father we
love

loving our
father

---

2   My aunt, Prisca Patterson, was named after my Filipina grandmother, Prisca Agsalud Guillermo. Like Saint Priscilla, the first woman presbyter, they, too, housed and raised would-be saints.

3   My father once told me the story of how they fell in love, that my mother would not stop chasing him in the hallway, teasing his long blond hippie hair and trying to braid them into pigtails, how he darted right into the bricks surrounding the fireplace. She offered to kiss his scraped arm, blood and all, and he let her. Then he said his lips hurt, too.

. . . and how The Mother's lips were the iron of his blood cracked open in the secret tuft of his cheek; the wind seeped through the chimney's cracks calling to him,

sam. come closer

wondered, was it the wind or that plastic bag of magic mushrooms, those dark tendrils in his back pocket; and then, in his right front pocket, that heavy hammer . . .

. . . and yea did the mourners form a circle, hands clasped out of forced habit; The GRAND FATHER led the first prayer as he had at a hundred funerals before . . .

loyalty and love

. . . mayhaps, The FATHER glared furiously[4] at the hypocrisy of the GRAND FATHER's words . . .

while he, the very reason

. . . thinking of LA, that land of gays and gangsters, the GRAND FATHER always called it . . .

danny ran away

. . . or mayhaps, The FATHER looked to the GRAND FATHER and felt pride that he had made the right choice, that danny had strayed from God's path . . .

demons in danny

the demons in all our hearts

succumbed succubus

---

4 My father was never the same after my uncle's death. Maybe it caused him to withdraw. Maybe he had to sacrifice part of himself, as one must let go of the devil.

. . . or mayhaps, The FATHER, in this moment of prayer, decided that he would never be like The GRAND FATHER, for The FATHER knew the secret of Nimrod, that first ruler sent from heaven to earth, the first ever patriarch . . .

mighty hunter be

. . . and that despite the prophecies and the thirteen books claiming otherwise, there was not an original thought in The GRAND FATHER's blimp of a head; The GRAND FATHER had merely copied his own FATHER, The GREAT GRAND FATHER, a farmer who worked ten-hour days and spent every night preaching on an AM radio show spreading the word of a god who would see them through the great depression . . .

fore the Lord began to be

mighty in the earth

. . . and too The GRAND FATHER's time in the navy during World War II was mere mirror simulation; The FATHER knew the truth behind that, too; how The GRAND FATHER had joined up after receiving a draft in the army and thusly took a coward's resignation by becoming a navy technician where the chances of seeing battle were severely lessened and the greatest war, for The GRAND FATHER, was a two-month visit to Shanghai prostitutes awaiting servicemen on R&R; the GI Joes who hadn't seen diddly-squat of an enemy were welcomed as war heroes under the soft-skinned squats of chinese girls . . .

fucked by survivors

of the nanjing massacre

. . . and thereupon was it The FATHER's turn to lead them in prayer, yet, despite being a preacher's son, dude couldn't pray for shit; there was an art to it; repeat the same question so they never question but feel

grandson's future home

uncomfortably exposed; make them feel guilty, asking for too much, and somewhat shocked or even offended that their small issues, which they had revealed in confidence, were made to sound grandiloquent . . .

. . . but when The FATHER was asked to pray he could conjure none of these talents;[5] he heard The GRAND FATHER speak first, and then went the other way with cliché after cliché after cliché . . .

. . . and yet The FATHER was effective for his own motives, that of not being the son cast away . . .

. . . and yea did The FATHER pray thinking of strippers refusing to get offstage when their song was up; friends peeked out and cleared their throats, but he held to the prayer with both hands, thumping ass on the prayer's base boards, straddling that prayer in midair, leg-locking, arms sweaty big and round, a professional sport, you know . . .

. . . thusly coaxed that fat prayer to death, torqued from pole to crucifix, until he heard whispers coming through that brick chimney, pleading in a concussive surge,

preachers have their way

of pettily making you

feel your pettiness

rubbed the ribbed

texture of the

hammer handle

dear god thank you for

this wonderful world full of

wonderful wonder

---

5 My father and I have the worst poker faces. We have a habit of shifting from wise to wiseass, as if every serious thought must be followed by an inexplicable fart, every stone platitude cracked.

sam. come outside. we're waiting for you

and thinking, was it God or danny or the shrooms who
spoke to him thus?

CHAPTER 2 VERSE 2

Wherein at the GRAND PARENTS' backyard woods THE FATHER is on hour three of mushroom tripping.

his brother mori

bound with morphine, wind swept by

said to him hello

lucent dust hovers

above frost-singed bush

and still webs wait

nd half-formed phrases littered The FATHER's mind; his breathing steadied while silence washed over; eyelids twitched, tongue clacked, the trees towered, the lung-shaped bark and liver-shaped bush silenced him; thinking, could he draw beauty from nourishment? . . .

. . . and yea how The FATHER walked for the same reason he jogged every morning, for solace beckoned onto the long trails of gravel and wood chips, a portal into tranquility . . .

. . . The FATHER's mind wavered with every step; his breathing slowed; he felt the dark din drowning out everything but his heartbeat; the unease of his chest, the seeping sweat . . .

. . . The FATHER gripped the hammer head; felt the cool iron magnetizing blood iron; O the anatomy of a hammer, begat . . .

a dry swamp of weeds

. . . how The FATHER cooled his face with its face, cheeked its cheek; eyed its eyehole, throated its throat, clawed his back right in the tired sores; what was an irish-man or a part-indigenous man without bruises and blood to wake up to; thus upon request The FATHER left the tool stillborn on the ground-level porch confettied in bits of funky blood, saith the hammer then,

gobbles up the old property

we plant corn for feed

     sam. leave me. sam

whereupon The FATHER heard his Mother Mary on the upper deck[1] surrounded by church ladies dressed for a hike not a wake; Mary shared memories of the depression, the days of picking cotton, sleeping on her big sister's linen sack while being dragged through the fields, slumbering gently . . .

every generation

those who tilled the soil for so long

had to be tilled themselves

---

1 My grandparents, Bill and Mary, bought the Gresham property in the 1970s, after they moved from Tennessee to Oregon. Quiet, on a hilltop, surrounded by evergreens and families of deer. Grandfather Bill gave his first sermons inside that house, practicing what he called "Christ-Centered Servant-Team Leadership," the name of one of his many educational workbooks, and the only one still in print.

... and one day The FATHER's Son would hear the same story and imagine an asteroid thousands of years in the future; Saint Christopher and his twin brother never should have been born, but no IUD birth control could stop the chosen ...

hands worn to toil;

... and the moss on a fallen tree was the hair on the arm of a dead brother; danny's arm, hammer cold and iron dead, and thinking, what the fuck was with his arm when it became hammer-cold and iron-dead? Did that arm turn slowly like turning off an oven? Did it last through the night or just an instant? Was it like coffee poured over ice? Was it mid-sentence? Mid-breath ...

bubbles of blood foamed

gurgles try to speak

... and how the self-flagellated, oozing wetness beneath his shirt, had him thus thinking, who the fuck cared for him in the end? Who the fuck used him like a tool in the end? ...

... and The FATHER thus waylaid into this feeling, ambushed by emotion behind a bush, felt that dark encircling and wondered when the ride would stop and that mounting desperation like he wanted to get off but ...

... too late thereof submerged beneath the waves of pain with those waves he merged ...

... until he heard the hammer whisper to him, no longer ready for use, but somehow, present still,

did he have a little brother
like himself
there at his bedside
when he died

did he have a young gay man
or a young gay woman
joining in the ranks
and acting up
when he died

I'm here all
alone

stay with
me danny
please I

can't go on
my own

did he let his gay friends
who called themselves family
use his decaying eyes
to fight their war on AIDS
was his body on full display
when he died

did he stay quiet
in defiance
of his catholic husband
and the gay predators
double his age
was he in a silent rage
when he died

smell of
sweaty fur

why did he die there
without the family
who had known him

odd when
that boy
peters out

bathed him
oh, and drove down
to LA

the one
folks talk
about

to try to save him
before he died

did those
hissing cymbals
make him take
the Lord's name
in vain
or was God there
to deliver him

resurgence
of life

from his pain
when he died

here in this
gap in the
woods

and thus was The FATHER rescued by the chime string
of a grasshopper he could not locate; and thusly did The

blue as
hydrangea

FATHER cross the event horizon, plateauing into that
spiritual afterglow . . .

while
heads
hooded in
judgment

. . . thusly did The FATHER imagine a last memory with
danny; holding him, hugging him so tight on the hospital bed and then the nurse said he was cutting off his air;

provoke
rebellion

and afterward danny was so winded but would not admit
his loss of strength and heaved and The FATHER felt he
had squeezed his brother too hard, that he

x
x
x
x
x

squeezed out of love a squeeze to last forever and now it would last forever; his brother's last words a sputter . . .

. . . how The FATHER[2] longed to know the names of the flowers, the ones the mourners brought; danny's favorite; what was it? . . .

. . . how he longed to know the color of ochre, how one exactly picked cotton, how lived the Native Americans[3] and the ways they worshipped before their roots were cleanly sheaved here in these woods . . .

. . . and thinking, there was no telling where the angels had lifted danny . . .

. . . and so The FATHER prayed there was some negotiation between them and the demons harboring inside his brother's soul; how The FATHER prayed that The Uncle had landed in a kind of purgatory, lonely still, because God was not there, but nevertheless, being purged . . .

the foundation of all

. . . and thereupon, The FATHER wondered if The Sons would remember loving The Uncle's lisp . . .

innocence is never having to question

one's own right to existence

---

2 Danny knew the secret of the world that my father could never know because my father never viewed his body as an object, as something desirable. He could not see the fog that abstracted and ornamentalized us.

3 My father knew not what it was to need a Supreme Court decision, or a martyr, or a song coded in rage, to prove that he was human.

. . . their visits to Los Angeles; got The FATHER thinking, oh no did he have AIDS when they visited? Did The Sons[4] use The Uncle's toothbrush? . . .

. . . and likewise The FATHER would take years to tell The Sons how The Uncle died, only that they should not want to end up like him; only Mother Mary would talk about him as one of the cuter ones . . .

he climbs
the ocean

tide he
strums our
shores

he pushes
and pulls

surfaced
undertow

---

4 I was not invited to the funeral. I was not invited to spread my uncle's ashes in the Pacific Ocean. Even in writing my father's pain, I cannot forget that at least he was invited to mourn. My memory is too blank to go on. And he's gone, so. Everything I know about him could be made up.

> when I die
> they'll do me in
> like they did to him
>
> when I die
> they will kill me
> again

what I write
and how

I write is
done in order

to save my
own life

> this page
> right here
> my fight to survive
>
> although I can't write
> for shit
> these days although
>
> no words emerge
> rests are still music
> silence still poetry

. . . thus afterglow fading, The FATHER picked clusters of blackberries for Mother Mary's pie; something to do while high; black slime climbed up his cold dead arm; blond blood trailed down his back, through the skinny pine . . .

. . . and what prowled through the dirt-scratched yard but a deer startled white then leapt back into the black . . .

hi your
high

ness I am

high as
fuck

. . . and The FATHER sat upon a compost bucket turned upside down in the thicket; dirt wet feeling himself sink at the pace of a sojourning heart, and heard that voice in the wind coo,

        sam come
        home kiss
        them all
        good bye

death

certain as
life, we

advance—

CHAPTER 3 VERSE 1

Wherein whilst drunken THE FATHER chooses not to come home he prefers to be an alcoholic anonymous.[1]

*will runs
deep*

*this tilled
spirit*

*sugar cane's
lash*

*the soothing
moans*

*of the
hypnotic
drones*

*glut with
what we
know*

we settin off

*a wordy
fusillade*

*for getting
laid*

i'm waiting for you sam

aid the paper cup of cheap Canadian rye that sat in the driver's-side cupholder while The FATHER drove on, flailing against the current; thinking, it's Friday! Or Tuesday? . . .

. . . either way, The FATHER had spent all day cleaning the kids' middle school; janitorial custodial, keeper of so many keys they weighed down his jeans . . .

. . . how some words just could not be accessed despite the many lexicons of knowledge a person could absorb . . .

. . . and the tide thus lapped The FATHER, the rearview mirror shouting,

let's scan some chicks

———————

1   By the time 1997 came around, my father had made oodles of enemies around town, each one extracted of all sympathy and dough.

and said The FATHER, shut up!

deaden your senses to
the dead around you

screeched the brake pedal, for no one can tell you the histrionics of when this binge began or when the waves will break . . .

. . . and yea how The FATHER remembered buying ice cream for the Sons,[2] his tears rank with hooch, thinking, there will be no ice cream in hell, they'll be on that rocky road all alone, crying, daddy, ice cream please . . .

. . . thus he found another bar, The Lucky Devil, south side of town, near his Step Daughter and her Son who lived without him and thus lived in sin; not so lucky devils . . .

_we deserved
it my_

_fatass
brother and
I and_

_our video
games and_

_my skin so
dark that no
one_

_would ever
believe_

_that my
father had
spawned me_

---

2 But I must have been a sight to see: long-haired androgynous brown kid so fat no one would believe that my little mother had birthed me.

I wore short shorts with very long T-shirts, way before it was K-cool. I realized only too late that my parents had no sense of fashion whatsoever, or worse, if they did, they had malicious intent in dressing me in extra-extra-large tie-dye T-shirts that puffed over my body like an air balloon. Strangers would ask if I was a girl or a boy and if I had showered recently and the answer to both was usually no.

Not to make excuses, but all this is to say, tldr: I might have abandoned me, too.

bar hopping
with the

island
hoppers
hopped up
at

the arcade
said the

passing iHop
sir, for you

I hope you
get back

on the band
wagon
though the

driver's
gotten off

. . . and The FATHER, hearing everywhere that his kids didn't look like him, that the black and filipina Step Daughter, whose black and indigenous hawaiian father, excuse me, kanaka maoli, just didn't bother . . .

. . . lips to that glass and eyes upon that stage, The FATHER got to thinking, were women happier back when they studied past issues of good housekeeping and tried to please a husband before being brainwashed by feminist hogwash, back when there was purpose and safety and Bibles and love and worship and songs and no one said a word about stroking your ego because ego was sin and we never believed we could know better than Him . . .

. . . and yea while he kept drinking he too kept thinking, coworkers and cats can't take care of you when you're elderly and don't get me started on affirmative action where's my affirmative action when will they stop trying to keep us poor are they trying to kill us? Might as well . . .

. . . binge; clock in; binge; clock out; binge; wife leaves; binge; she's probably out with some guy; binge; come home late; binge; drink the scope; binge; jack off to catalogs; binge;[3] and The Son finds it later; binge; creased at the lingerie section, binge; feel weird . . .

---

3 Mid-nineteenth century: from English dialect *binge* "to soak a wooden vessel."

. . . now down the rye stored in the toilet bowl; binge; find yourself clever as if no one knows; binge; deal with The Step Daughter; binge; who fucking hates you; binge; watch her cut you from your own; binge; grandson's life; binge . . .

. . . she's all, bitch; binge; don't ever call him; binge; your grandson . . .

. . . now read the Bible in the living room; binge; swig on the toilet; binge; binge classes; binge; always back to fat cans; binge; make sure it's you taking out the bottles for recycling; binge; in the neighbor's cans; binge; no fuck that walk to the 7-11; binge; no shame; binge; life's a game; binge; we binge watch . . .

. . . now saunter home; binge; spill your stomach; binge; onto the boys' bed; binge; fight with the mrs.; binge; scream so the kids can hear; binge; always in their room; binge; playing games; binge; with themselves . . .

. . . no; binge; throw a plate at the floor; binge; punch a hole in the wall; binge; maybe she loves someone else cuz; binge; why the fuck would anyone at all; binge; still love you after all the . . .

upon our

manila
hemp

craft we
binge

birds bring

bearded
bros

to binge

binge

let the old
oak

soak

binge

so well you

swell

binge

bring being
beneath the

bridge

CHAPTER 3 VERSE 2

Wherein whilst drunken THE FATHER never wants to come home he prefers to be a bro ho.[1]

f all The FATHER's strip club shits, this one looked like scrambled eggs, and it was around breakfast time too . . .

. . . whenst later in the same bathroom the dancer's thighs revved up his engine's junked-up testicles, screaming to life a lust once disguised as humiliation . . .

island
women
make

. . . thus did The Mother say divorce just as he was getting back on the wagon, just as he was starting to go back to school; MA in education; finally some direction, but that little islander golddigger . . .

good wives

whatever
happens
they've

. . . and thus did The FATHER desire to kill himself, thus did he make the threat, and thus still The Mother threatened to leave, find a new man to raise The Sons, wolfing down on his balls; so what if The FATHER goes to strip clubs, has the occasional girl on call . . .

seen worse

mother born
to fight

sister devoid
of mercy

father can
you hear me

---

1 By the time 1998 came into focus, my father had memorized six stripper's birthdays, gifted nine pocket rockets to community college girls around town, each one cleaning out his sympathy and his dough.

... empty was the glass in front of him; thus he ordered another and a moment later, empty too was that glass; thus he ordered two more; disappear too did those glasses, every time ...

snatch conversation

her hair her air her despair

... and yea did she spirit The FATHER to the sub-rosa underground where, bottle-blind, he felt her miscolored eyes, one dirt brown and one grass green, roam up and down his face, and the fertilized dirt saying,

how he gonna pay?

      like what you see?

spoiled by glimpses

... likewise The FATHER introduced her to the carnal ca-boose and got fucked in the family van, slipping his wafer tongue into her rosebud mouth; bubbles of gas bouncing to their awkward rhythm ...

an assault on the senses

sparking rods and cones

... and yea, how then The FATHER knew his skin never truly touched hers yea and that his tongue never truly got lost in her mouth yea for it was ordained that people can never really touch each other yea because on a microscopic level yea there is no real touch just a minuscule yea unsee-able yea empty space between bodies yea so it can't really be cheating (yay!) ...

eyelashes fan like

dark feathers above her cheeks

... and how The FATHER knew that sex was only in the mind; thinking yea, the real cheater was not he, but The Mother, who cheated not with the untouching of skin, but with the taking of bread and a betraying heart ...

flash mirthless half-smile

fire crackles
dance up
her face

like a colicky

child with
nothing to
lose and

going for
baroque

. . . and how The FATHER knew he wasn't dumb, how he knew this girl, love her as he may, was not for keeps; thus was spoken to him by the bouncer, and the full-blathered fifty he gave her . . .

. . . and how The FATHER knew this, how he did not flutter when she flapped off that full-bladdered rubber and delivered herself from his privy chambers . . .

her bare
burning bulb

bobbed in
his direction
go

ahead dive
deep and
swim

CHAPTER 3 VERSE 3

Wherein whilst drunken THE FATHER never wants to come home he's a curse hanging around THE FAMILY[1] and the MOTHERFUCKER knows it.

Now The FATHER entered his empty home, fixed and flipped by the real estate agent with a fresh coat of paint to cover the booze stains, putty to fill in the fist-shaped holes, caulk to replace his manhood . . .

. . . and there was no one home but that dog barking in the backyard and that fridge full of grape juice and those drawers of stale crackers and with them The FATHER made his communion without the commune . . .

. . . for The FATHER knew how to manipulate the flock, how to crawl back to The GRAND FATHER's house with a tearful confession,[2] how to tug the words, who hurt our baby blue eyes? Was it that islander slut? The mafia comare

*my head
bobs above*

the water

*but the hand
of the*

hurricane

*pushes it
down down*

---

1 By 1999, we'd had enough of his decline. He'd crossed every red line in the sand, run out of time, and we'd had enough of his bullshit changes.

2 My grandfather started some nasty rumors about my mother when we left. That she had entered a life of sin. That she was addicted to drugs. That she fell in love with a gangster in Las Vegas. Strange nonsense packaged into emails and canonized into the mailboxes of true believers.

kidnapping the kids? Sue her! Ring up child services! Get the kids back! She's raising them in an immoral environment[3] . . .

. . . now The FATHER sauntered up the staircase to the master bedroom to the forgotten dryer and took from within that purple dress; off-shoulder; optional spaghetti strap; and thought of the thousand times he had slipped his hand beneath it, how he had raised its fabric, and how it didn't seem fair that just days ago he could lean his head on her thighs as they watched tv in bed; and now she's saying never again,

> asked the FATHER
>> why do you see
>> the world
>> in black and
>>> white?

> answered The GRAND FATHER
>> because
>>> it is

W
O
O
F
!

to save
brown
women

from brown
men

ya gotta lift
them

again and
again

from the soil

---

3 I often wonder why my mother took so long to extract us from that house. But then I think of her. A brown woman, with two light-skinned brown sons, and a Black and Indigenous daughter who had her own Black and Indigenous son. Where could such a family, with children birthed from three different broke and broken fathers, flee?

and how The FATHER felt that the true hell of divorce[4] was in his fingers never again tracing the warm contours of her body . . .

. . . thereupon in the bathroom his features stiffened; he needed something to quell the rage; can't find no tall cans; she found them all on her way out the cunt the cunt the cunt how dare she the . . .

. . . and there upon the empty toilet tank did The FATHER smile at the mirror, and thereupon his crooked teeth, bald-eagle head, and despairing eyes did he punch the mirror, and thereupon after five years of taekwando, still couldn't throw a punch for shit, thereupon the glass was intact, with not a hairline fracture . . .

. . . thereupon did The FATHER cleanse the house, rompin' stompin' around, driving out the plates and glasses and mugs and the VCR and anything of her touch, assured that this den of robbers had forced him to do it . . .

W
O
O
F
!

*most men
don't show
their*

*grief or their
sadness you
know*

*in fact most
rage most*

anger is just

*the cork that
keeps all the
grief*

in the bottle

------

4 Both of my grandfathers were hardline preachers. Their congregations remained small because they refused to compromise. The third commandment was not the only eternal sin. There was homosexuality. There was worshipping false gods, including the false god of Catholicism. And there was divorce. Of all these sins, the sin of divorce was the most controversial. My grandfathers, time and again, lost their flock, and their families, separating the righteous from the hell-bound divorcees.

W
O
O
F
!

W
O
O
F
!

since I spake
I cried

out I cried
violence and
spoil

because the
word of

the LORD
was made a
reproach

unto me and
a

derision
daily.

. . . now this the house of prayer, this the house of The FATHER who bore a family, this the brick porch, this the backyard of rose bushes and strawberry pits that like The Family borne would stay away long after the sun had scorched each bottle dry and the rains had washed the vomit trails away and on that day The Family would pass by the old house and look in disgust and pity and fear for their former selves; whispering to the past, run[5] . . .

. . . thereupon would come a day that only The FATHER would ever look fondly upon the home and remember the story of Job, the average Joe, who didn't understand why God cursed his birth and thereupon would The FATHER pray for his brother's soul saying,

God please stop testing me
why is she cursing me
divorcees can't go to heaven
why is she doing this
to my soul

W
O
O
F
!

5 My mother, at some point, got tired of waiting for an opportunity to come along. Over many years, she put together a national network of people working in aviation who began to meet at an annual conference that she herself ran. Some call her the aviation mother, the one whose brain birthed community, who told pilots where to go. But she knew that someday soon she would need friends in faraway places.

now with fingers caressing a dark-skinned troll of purple
fuzzy hair, one of The Mother's dozens; dark crusted
blood besmirched the purple fuzz . . .

. . . and that dog won't stop barking . . .

. . . if there was another place . . .

. . . and time . . .

. . . another family . . .

. . . and that dog won't stop barking!

W
O
O
F
!

*leave the
mutt out
cold*

W
O
O
F
!

*no food no
water*

W
O
O
F
!

*neighbors
call the
pound*

W
O
O
F
!

*to take him
away*

ALL OUR YELLOW FEVERS

CHAPTER 4 VERSE 1

sun

gusts of lament and

griefs of cloud shroud past

a thinning footpath

For though The FATHER knew that The GRAND FATHER would never approve of him going to this megachurch of instruments and plasma TVs and an entire canteen for the half-ass believers . . .

. . . still he remained in this ornate land of false prophets, Las Vegas . . .

. . . and how now, 2002, three years after the divorce, The Sons' souls[1] had no better chance in this fight . . .

---

not characters but

brief avatars for the shades

phasing in and out

of fat but nimble digits

1 I lived in the clouds long before The Cloud. My kindergarten teacher reported worries about me standing in the corner talking to my hands, naming them, making "pshh pshh" sounds in some alien language.

By the time I was a teenager, I had learned to enter the cloud at will. I spent Sundays with my father sitting in this Las Vegas megachurch, obedient yet absent, eyes on the collar-shirted preacher, not hearing a word of his sermon. Sometimes, during a chorus of claps, I would look at my attentive father and think how nothing in my imagination could help me understand how he spent all day doing the right thing just before phasing into the skeeviest guy imaginable.

. . . and there befell upon the city its expunged stars[2] . . .

---

2   Hold up, sorry. There's still more, cuz if I'm being honest,
around this time in Las Vegas, my father's troubles were well
eclipsed by my own. He had moved to Las Vegas to be with us, an
unexpected and kind gesture, but I can barely remember him being
there. Because that was also the time that I befriended some racist
fucking people.

If I'm being terribly honest, I remember one of them, when I was
driving and he was riding shotgun, saw a group of Black children
and called them "little niglets." My friends and I, in also a joking
tone, told him he was racist as hell. We car of friends who only
ate from the dollar menu at Jack in the Crack would often com-
pete to say the most shocking and repulsive thing, being young and
trying out new words, testing their impact, experimenting with
their magical power and discovering just how much we could get
away with.

we all just

trying to leave

a mark

If I'm being terribly terribly honest, one of my friends showed
signs of racism that went well beyond our dark magic lexicon.
Having grown up in a nearly all-white Christian school and spending only enough time in Hawai'i to not be called a tourist, I had no
shared knowledge of what collective racial struggle looked like. To
say I was ill equipped is no excuse, though I also cannot remember a single discussion about race or colonization even at my public
school, which was majority people of color, in a city that was majority brown. Even so, I could not see that one of my best friends
was a fully committed white supremacist whose skinhead older
brother served as a district police officer.

see them

your readers

thirsty

onlookers

how they

Only years later did this realization wash over me. After I had taken
classes in African American literature. After I had scraped together
enough of my family's generational memory. Only then did I learn
that my friend was there on a particular night when a group of white

love to watch

you change

can

I

live

?

even to
declare

that I'm
writing
for myself

would still
mean I'm
plead

ing to make
meaning from
this

mighty
mud slung
ball

supremacists canceled an AfroLatino activist—that is, shot and killed him in the desert. When I heard the story, I was long out of Las Vegas, and it was something like learning about a massacre in the Middle East by US military forces, both astonishing and inevitable.

I was enraged, and my anger was aimed less at my old friend and more at myself. How did I not see the inevitable? I hadn't seen him in many years, so I looked him up on Facebook. More inevitability. He had become a police officer, just like his brother. Unsatisfied with patrolling the streets of Las Vegas, he had taken a job in Detroit "to clean up the city streets."

Every moment I spent with him I could have opened my eyes and learned something. And at every opportunity to do so, I failed.

I had yet to understand any of this back when I was a teenager sitting next to my father in a Las Vegas megachurch. Yet some loose strains of inevitability had begun to develop like pale arteries. I saw in the church things I could not articulate, traditions I could not evade. The words of a preacher, trilling and seductive, are not hard to suss out. It clear-cuts the open veins of bigotry when a preacher has to justify how God's early followers raped women and massacred children. Church made inevitabilities as clear as blood on leaves. Clear: the person I would become were I to keep floating toward the pearly gates.

Religion, my father, my racist friends, at some point, all had to go. And it just so happened to happen in that order.

CHAPTER 4 VERSE 2

cloud

Thereupon did The FATHER drive The Sons around the city, and thereupon did they once again question The FATHER's questionable taste in music; The Eagles and Garth Brooks and the JB that was always somewhere in the queue . . .

. . . it happened that long after they'd gotten used to the casinos and the megachurches and the desert temptations and the dry-aired mesas and the sprawling two-story houses color coded in tan and dark tan . . .

las vegas

closes
around you

lion's jaw

. . . that The Sons[1] spoke of breaking the cardinal sin, which had The FATHER thinking, why do they call it cardinal? Try a dad joke. For some people, heaven just ain't in the cards[2] . . .

---

1 I was a likable enough chance, though I no longer believed God gave you liberation. God granted men control. Fathers over daughters. Husbands over wives. Whites over everyone else.

2 It was apparent to my brother and me that my father had moved to Las Vegas for the cardinal reason of saving our souls. If some parents spoke in a love language of tasty food, my father spoke love through the reminders that there existed a brutal, isolated hellscape ready to smother us in ash.

...thrice upon this car ride did The FATHER think how he longed to note the notes, like The Son on the guitar,[3] his ear tuned to notation; how The FATHER felt so out of tune, how he lived in inversed verses ...

marry brown

and here comes the

brother hood

...how time threaded by; how's your job?; threading reels in booths;[4] saying nothing on the way to a home that The FATHER had never stepped foot in; at least silence protected him from feeling battered by words; the punishing conversations that left him mentally brittle, those saccharine voices that put him at a grim distance, radiating cheer and happiness, until one day ...

...And yea did The Son, herald of the traveling saint, Saint Christopher, plug his walkman into the car stereo, and yea to a slurry song did he sing along,

> "I have no belief
> but I—"

---

3 When I was fourteen, I flipped a coin to decide if I was going to be a writer or a musician. If my parents' divorce wasn't the best thing that ever happened to me, that coin landing on heads surely was.

4 When we turned fifteen, my brother and I began working for a movie theater, scrubbing floors and fishing out soiled discard from beneath cinema seats. We made $5.50 an hour and worked there for years, coming of age, graduating, falling in and out of love. We never questioned this life, which was to be our lives, we thought, for the rest of our lives. And to this life, perhaps, may we someday return.

"—but you
don't really mean that
do you?"

the question dwarfed them, The Son's eyes saying, I don't
know . . .

. . . and maybe The Son didn't know whether or not he
knew, but he did, and The FATHER saw it, and both
brooded, and brooded . . .

. . . and mayhaps they settled upon the same fear that
no matter how much thought they gave, clarity's charity
would never come . . .

when it
came to the
games

of white boy
whining

how long do
you figure

it took him
to figure

we were no
longer

rooting for
the same
team?

CHAPTER 4 VERSE 3

storm

 nd thus stood The Mother, ice queen of ice cream, dark silhouette . . .

. . . The FATHER got out of the car; kids scuttled back to the house . . .

. . . and how with anxiety sheltered behind an officious smile did The FATHER rock back on his heels; thus had the time come; pressure cooker . . .

he chases her across the sky

. . . and as he summoned the strength to turn his head, her gaze racked him over; force-pushed his hands against the wall . . .

orion and taurus, glisten and seethe

. . . on second thought, The FATHER faced that firing squad; The Mother's honeyed smile lingered at The Sons, but at him her lips curled in distaste, at him her eyes narrowed, at him she took measure . . .

together sink away

. . . and how her cleanliness only reminded The FATHER of his own dried-out eyes, his own ale-soured breath, his own face suffused with inebriation, his own droopy lips . . .

. . . thus did The FATHER clear his throat, see himself wince, his jaw tighten, the clouds that battered the sky like bruises, and yea did his white Ford speak forth,

      did you not
      drive all this way
      from your puny studio apart
      ment on the other
      side of town?

but it's too

damn late
her heart
has flown

far away

Thus did The FATHER behold the stubborn earthiness of her skin, thus did he imagine how good life had been to her, how in this world of diversity and affirmative action it must have been nice for every action to be so affirmed . . .

die verse
city

while grief
and war

. . . how for The Mother's entire life the world had wanted to be her friend . . .

just clamor
on

. . . that The Mother wouldn't even allow him to take the kids out past dark, into the darkness, when he might— what? leave them at an arcade? . . .

words flung
from

her mouth
like dirt
scattered

. . . for so saith the Ford,

      but are you drunk
      right now?
      no you are
      just furious

      you're the one
      who came all this way

from a
spade

I will

kill him if he
touches

my kids

I will

kill myself if
they

go astray

"you're
looking—"

but it's

too damn
late

got this job
just so she

could presume
you're still a drunk
should've tossed yourself
through the windows

and the sting of The Mother's back was acid corroding
down his inner body . . .

. . . and it may not have mattered to him then that his Son
Saint Christopher would one day remember this moment
while reading the words of the novelist Jesmyn Ward about
a young girl at the throat of her lover,

this is
Medea

wielding
the knife

this is Medea

cutting

CHAPTER 4 VERSE 4

rain

as Vegas lights glimmered in the rain or was it The FATHER's inebriated merry-go-round of sharp winces of pain that spoke to him in a chorus saying he deserves the true name,

> tk tk tk tk yes
> tk tk tk tk you
> tk tk tk tk god's
> tk tk tk tk son

and yea while traffic crawled, the saturated streets caught the downpour concealing those monuments to the grizzle made ethereal in neon purples and pinks; a quick wave of nausea and said the gas pedal,

> time's up
> but you ain't
> time's bitch

in the light of the Luxor beam, the sky black as sloe, the brake pedal did say,

> the only way
> to be together
> is To-Get-Her

women and children

all over the world want men

to die

so that they can live

and thus saith the gearshift,

> you'll feel better
> ye just crash crash
> and you're out
>
> you'll survive
> ye airbags bags
> and you're god

alone
a boat

adrift
aslant

and lo, a striking woman in a glistening raincoat of drop-
lets shining; the rain saying, you're being tested,

empty
and whole

> tk tk tk tk you
> tk tk tk tk turn
> tk tk tk tk fish

and the drops of alcohol in his bloodstream reflected in
the rear-viewing mirror got him thinking, when The Sons
get over eighteen, no need to stick around to see what she
does, no more being bled out for child support . . .

the wagon

. . . The FATHER too could tune out like a weathervane

on the boat

committing to wherever the wind blew, wind saying,

cast at sea

> you lost
> go—
> god is always part of
> yo—
> you don't feel him

anymo—

did you lose
god   this is
                                           Medea
because you feel
depression   wielding the
                                           knife
anger
or are
anger
depression   this is
                                           Medea
what you feel because
god   cutting
is what you lost?

tk tk tk tk she
tk tk tk tk turn   this is
                                           Medea
tk tk tk tk cheer
                                           wielding the
she'll do better   knife
she just forgot got
her sins

your kids   this is
                                           Medea
support
open veins   cutting

sam come
restraining order against
the sun

this is
Medea
tonight let rain

slate down your throat

love rain slake thirst reflect

this is
Medea
the shining stabs of moon

light shivs and the water falls

a bene diction

this is
Medea

this is
Medea

this is
Medea

this is
Medea

this is
Medea

this is
Medea

CHAPTER 4 VERSE 5

cane

T hus did The FATHER . . .

. . . come home to a rain . . .

. . . soaked mattress . . .

. . . forgot he had . . .

. . . been airing it out . . .

. . . for mites . . .

. . . left it in the . . .

. . . sun . . .

. . . turned to down . . .

. . . pour . . .

drift bed

lump
wool

get older

teach
middle

schoolers
too

little pay

side jobs

can't afford

studio squat

can barely

make the

ends meet

pay the

up keep

pray and

pray and

and pray

and pray

... and thus barely a crack was made when The FATHER again punched the walls ...

have you
ever run

... and not a chance had The FATHER of shattering the mirror glass just himself shattered in rain ...

out in a
thunderstor
m and

... and how The FATHER wept and wept ...

kissed the
rain? it
takes

... and at four-twelve in the morning The FATHER would have run into the rain, fly unzipped, arms flailing ...

... if he did not see that shade; if he did not know he was still mourning the boy, the man ...

everything
in me not to

run out to
kiss you

... the slithers of clouds at dusk, the candy-cane sky ...

... The FATHER would not know, would not care that ...

danny. I'll
stay on this
path

... The Son Saint Christopher would one day imagine this moment ...

not to say
that word

... while reading the words of Jesmyn Ward, who wrote of relentless pain,

that

like each

unbearable
day

it

will dawn

x
x
x
x
x

A PSALM OF MY MOTHER, WHO, AFTER FIVE YEARS DIVORCED, RETURNS TO PORTLAND

I· The Diodyssey

never in my life did I
ever see my mother cry
she would drive while I held maps
her face igneous surface dried
upon time's coarse wind we'd ride
I knew she had tears inside
cold glades to fill in the gaps

I imagine her, perhaps
treading Hawthorne's underside
streets repaved, arctic wind snaps
sprays of anarchic tenor
archaic signs remember
arrows that quiver in flight
once, she shivered at the site

now, white eyes fall like dripped wax
light the flags that flap that fall
like his twitch when slept too late
flaring brain of cortisol
blurred and worn his psalms berate

palm trees palmed, another lapse
less and less she called it fate

now, eyes light through membrane caul
this not-Portland, same named street
new color, different drumbeat
grungers with fresh wherewithal
sun pinches a wooden fence
dropping copper at their feet
new era to reel in scents

walking cure to build her core
she'd never done this before
write, then stand, then speak out loud
for a conference she'd mentor
kids and trays birthed from her brain
fueled and dispatched an airplane
through a stratus mother cloud

birth a cauliflower crowd
garlic cloves spun from her vein
what the husband said allowed
each their own motioned weather
she the warmth, the high pressure
tropic wind shakes windowpane
low hills house a hurricane

her humidity a shroud
for the sunset's languished glow

balm of a circling tempest
from magic island hilo
how long, how long, since she'd guess
whether, up in heaven's cloud
her Apong: tenants, or guests?

O! The migrant calypso!
She who hitched up God's sanctum!
She that witch summons phantoms!
Fire-lit hounds who overflow!
Too long, too long, since that thought:
Apongs' souls held for ransom
by his cruel, tallied onslaught!

II· The Momnet

Oh mother, summer, her hands my hands, look:
dark digits, tree bark scarred from posters for
missing kids and pets. She lands in a nook
at Bagdad Theater's mosquitoed outdoor.
They soar to drink a drunk's sinewy corps
their hirsute chests, undone shirts, she could guess
that nimrods were inept beasts of folklore
and bugs could get drunk from their happiness.

Vodka martini on happy hour!
"Be right with you," the waiter's sly come-on
balking her bulwarks, climbing her tower

perhaps after, a shoulder to cry on?
She felt her core thrash, a fish on a hook
All that blooms must fall says the holy book.

O mother, alone, lax, but not knocked down
among haloed haoles she finds a chair
and grips a martini glass, fingers brown
that flip the pages and leaf her black hair
as whiskey's whisked scent lilts in from elsewhere
from a caparisoned man playing sax
above the grainy and gray static square.

Brass speaks sotto voce, "please" to climax
a moan that tears, tears, tears, tears, tears the air.
His name was once her dowry, Guillermo:
the wife weaving lies, the daughter and heir
to a friar and Chinese mestizo.
Ever priests, ever leased, ever the gown.
Eyes web in-bound. Was this ever their town?

O mother, under tables her calves cleave
while on drooped petal-cloths of maimed carmine
she tries to write a lecture, to conceive
of words—no huh howzit brahs, no talkin'
story, no Flip's philippic chismis pidgin—
no talk! Words would bring thought into being.

Too fast for the web, talk gave permission
to catch up and not be caught, the beaming
forward, hammering past time, some da kine

their meet of balmed sweat, his freeze before her
the climate swells, the heron squalls, the tide
of kai begins to turn, pulses with a blur
and petal masks of tenderness deceive
if autumn always browns the leaves—then *leave!*

O mother sprung, she left, she made a split.
A sinecure for sin, make no mistake
that pliant as a plant, right here she'll sit
and shed memories like leaves in an earthquake
a bit each day, filling in the black lake
and from gray clouds she'll drink the yellow sun
and write: the IUD, the scar, the ache
call him the sperm donor, the race long run!

Pen in hand, finally, a moment breaks
to touch a rose and see it start to sag
she lights with sparkles and in brilliance takes
water from bare cracks, color from a flag:
"Take to the skies, find a house, and end it
twelve years, two kids *before* you ended it!"

III· Ode to Dionysus

O Mother Drink! Caught in life's glue
always late, we took time to chew
worshipping our own presence
the sting of the vague adventure

the dull of the morning after
presenting each our essence

she sails through stargazer lilies
and lit black candle melodies
in a dirge her waves pursue
the wails of the dark theater
where she sits and hears familiar
notes dissolving to a tune

here, screen-flickers form glares and shades
they flare, then ebbed in dark, she fades
to Dionysian rapture
when songs, tunes, chants, were but denounced
her muted mutiny pronounced
the day she would flee capture

back then, getting out seemed too hard
it ate her soul to leave him scarred
had she appraised all the ways?
without the lies or betrayal?
definitionless, unstable
now, no longer wrapped in leis!

husband, we drank our own poison
deadened presence to illusion
preachers without a choir
alone, we fought beleaguered skies
alone, until our battle cries
echoed back to the crier

what more reason could mother list
then some hearts never could resist
taking, buying, keeping close
ornamental marginalia
just read the cargoed scholia!
His-tory we de-compose!

So, immaterial dark we drink
ashy freedom of life unlinked
we, ourselves, in banishment!
And in darkened theaters we weep
like stripped rubber sap our tears seep
we, no one's embellashment!

we dig musubi from our purse
with our toes, flip off our converse
dry off the soggy lessons
we drink up, no more to undo
our feet up, no more anti-you
and we gift our presence

TO HELL AND BACK TO HELL AGAIN

CHAPTER 6 VERSE 1

gtfo or die[1]

her elliptical

had long passed into someone

else's constellation

he plodded on, moon

in attendance it would be

six hundred years more

of speculation til his

sky saw another

heavenly body

Upon the airplane to South Korea or whenever he decided to give up on America and give in to the rise of Asia, The FATHER found himself believing he could start over, thinking, fuck this family, this country, child support has killed me, attachment is killing me . . .

. . . no longer wedding ringed, The FATHER winced whenever The Sons[2] called him by his name,[3] but here it was like a constant blaring horn before an executioner released the floor out from under him; how even the local Koreans and snarky expats thought it rude . . .

---

1 In 2006, my father was the first in my family to leave the US for a reason other than war or a vacation. No one else even had a passport. Some believed my father ran away.

2 Later that year, my brother and I followed him to South Korea. I stayed for eight months. My brother never left.

3 To this day I still wonder why we joined him. Did we want to give him a second chance? Did we enjoy watching him break down before our eyes? Or did we see how he lived, $2,000 a month, free healthcare, beauty everywhere, and wonder if brown boys, too, could thrive upon someone else's grace?

...and The FATHER hated being called The American, yet his song of choice at every noribang was Born in the USA ...

...and perhaps The FATHER had learned from one star-struck mistress to another to be playful yet inspired; true sabishi, spiritual loneliness, mu and zen[4] ...

...thus to The FATHER this tribal thinking never changed, this identity straight-jacketing, that even here in a nation high-jacked by American warships and high on American worship people still corralled into national choirs ...

...no[5] intuition ...

...no guts ...

...no gut feeling ...

my
supercilious
father

reflected on
etymologies

of bitter &
guilty

while I
began to lift
the lid

of queer &
quirky

the two of
us angry

and super
silly

---

4 My father's desire to transcend his own whiteness peaked while in Korea. But this time it was not directed at the Black and brown family members who betrayed him, nor to the students who mocked him, but to the Koreans who labeled him. While his two sons grappled with being seen as Filipino in Korea, he would always read as American. Thus, American was his new thing to escape, rather than whiteness. Or, rather, an Americanness that was always white.

5 My father carried a power in Korea that gave argument to his ecclesiastical leanings: transoceanic working-class coalition.

here there
is no need

for school
janitors

students
janitor
themselves

... buzz buzzed an expat English teacher,

and he still

    the collectivist

loved her

    mindset means their collectives

pathetically

    feel not guilt but shame[6]

and he still

shame[7] on their face when The Sons called The FATHER

reminisced

Sam ...

upon her

... shame,[8] shame[9] The FATHER could understand ...

pathetically

time

for another

phlegmatic

dirge

so

pathetic

this love

---

6 Because he's known poverty.

7 And too: religious solidarity.

8 And too: sin.

9 And too: deliverance.

CHAPTER 6 VERSE 2

level ten saint

itting within the creaky pews of that Yoido megachurch, The FATHER heard but could not listen to The Preacher's Korean sermon, so he thought respectfully of the night before[1] at that pisswater cocktail bar where they spin bottles and light your shit on fire, where The FATHER screamed at a waitress in front of The Sons; called her a whore and threw cash at her feet, saying, this money is all you want, my money; and The FATHER was all ready to throw a conniption but she didn't get the joke, saying, I just asked for liquor not I want to lick her, just a joke you edgy wannabe, and by the way is your name Anastasia, cuz you a nasty asia . . .

he claimed never

to remember

what was inconvenient

to remember

. . . and it was unclear whether The Sons loved him or just loved watching him die inside or if one was secretly writing a book about him; how they certainly did love to debate him to death, to CRUSH his YouTube conspiracy theories; how they must have loved to hear him

always ailing

always aleing

---

1 My father began to understand that eternal paradox of being a father, that despite his love for his sons, he could never be their friend. He would always be the thing they went to their friends to complain about.

our
existence
kept

my father
from ending

his life

this is not to
say

we gave
purpose to

his life

pounding on their door the night before, knocking screaming straining; people came out to the hallway to stare at him sleeping there . . .

. . . and was it really a big deal, sleeping on the floor, it's where the heating comes, you know; lulled to sleep by the floor's heat, no need to stay awake til four-twelve, the ghost hour, only wake from abrupt bouts of his gout-bulbed toes . . .

. . . and in the noise of The Preacher's tongue, The FATHER found a peaceful ease,[2] a sonic meditation of air con that sent the mind drifting to how the black-haired heads of so many people no longer seemed strange . . .

. . . and how even their stares were no longer birds chirping at the foreign phantom, the ground walker, the English sounding board, the drain that all the duckies swirled around . . .

for fifteen
years

my family
sang

the only non
white people

in a white
church

---

2   The one time I made it to church in Korea, I saw three levels of congregates sluicing spit onto their phones believing that the ceiling lights, seen through a blurred camera, gave the adorers a "faithfulness score." That day, the preacher had just come back from a two-month "talk to god" in Thailand. God had told him that President Kennedy was assassinated because he did not give enough money to the church. And also, gay people died of HIV because they did not give enough money to the church. And also, Black people were oppressed because they did not give enough money to the church.

x
x x
x x x
x x x x
x x x x x

. . . and how after a year The FATHER felt blessed to be there, poor but rich with friends, here with no white men with rich lives and kind wives . . .

. . . here where his self-destructive mourning established kinship with the men around him, where getting drunk and passing out in alleys in red-flushed screams and breaking things was not so uncommon, where extreme tastes were in the sharp honesty of gochujang; The FATHER loved it all, loved the people and their ability to forgive without apology[3] . . .

. . . and it was thus at the sermon's end that the entire parish stood to take pictures of the ceiling to count the echelons of its opaline solarium and to speak in tongues and to squeeze their bodies and to heave . . .

. . . and it was thus among the rapt audience that The FATHER had no time for a glib comment or to comment upon the mad glint in his eyes, still hung over her . . .

. . . until he saw her, another her; a white scarfed apostle, eyes brimming from above her phone . . .

for four
years

my father
prayed

the only
non-Korean
person

in a Korean
church

if a white
daddy

falls in a
forest

of bamboo
trees

would
anyone

anyone

notice the
wood?

----

3 Having escaped the blasé progressivisms of the Pacific Northwest and the in-your-face multiracisms of Las Vegas, my father decided to stop fucking around with identity politics. Here, in a land of Asian faces, you could really come into your own non-Asianness.

CHAPTER 6 VERSE 3

breathe

*my father
adored*

*by the
church
ladies*

T hen at the after-service potlatch of tea and snacks, The FATHER learned again to covet; the sin that was not sinful, thinking, to covet was to convert and thus was not really a sin . . .

*bald head
too tall*

. . . and thus this sin of many names in a foreign land mayhaps could not yet be called imperial . . .

to be seen

*empty
wallet*

*man of
substance*

*old-ass
phone*

. . . and how the women were obscenely attractive even in their conservative white and yellow dresses; how freshly laundered, freshly pressed, freshly shining skin, luminescence of grace, woke him back to the whispers of the white tag left up on a woman's yellow collar,

*no
allowance*

know

*gigantic
hands*

her words blind you

no

*a possible
kink*

her words bind you

*his inability
to cook*

and yea how The FATHER knew while stirring that cup of sugary nescafé it was not coffee but fake coffee with a dollop of fake milk; thinking, were they trying to make his superiority so easy . . .

*a job
opening*

... here where no one knew of The FATHER's ignoble past,[1] here where a man like him could cruise around as he pleased ...

... and thus approached the white scarfed woman peeking through her fingers to block the sun blots through the windows; she too became transfixed, she a cram school student whose chipped white fingernails insisted, this is coffee ...

nights she stayed at church

... and how in well-versed English she encouraged his perception; saying, analogue, collectivist, repressive, patriarchal, neo-Confucian, though one never finds the analects here ...

til morning, her faith level

at fifty percent

... and how The FATHER encouraged the church women to cathect because that's what Jesus would do and how The FATHER never really had the chance to play the role of Jesus before with all those other Jesuses in the room ...

---

1 We felt free to become different people in Korea. I had no taste for coffee, but when I introduced myself as a coffee savant, no one denied my unbreakable love for everything caffeine.

all I did was say

I invested in an espresso machine. I made pains to insert my Seattle cred, to scoff at every Starbucks cup. Coffee gave me an edge, a shield from ridicule.

arab ica! and

My father, however, came shipped with shield and armor all included.

words became magic

. . . thinking, but here in the eastern choir, cathect ya
damn well could . . .

his face

his words

his charm

his raw top

energy

wet as

lukewarm

ji gae

CHAPTER 6 VERSE 4

deify

nd thereupon did The FATHER walk with the white scarfed woman in Gimhae's[1] humidity, indulge her, try to forget how her name, August, was like . . .

. . . and it was August who took The FATHER up tarmac-laden paths, past the soccer fields, past Yeonji Park, past the Homeplus, past the large factory of fertilizer stink, past the stares of iceberg observation, thinking, were they his students or her family members . . .

. . . and it was at the tomb of King Suro where August told The FATHER of the Indian princess Suriratna later Queen Heo Hwang-ok from whom over six million Koreans proudly descend . . .

. . . and it was there that The FATHER declared Korea a world operating on olfactory location; thus proven in the sewer waste near his hagwan, the aromatic waffle vendors, the samgyupsal, the soju mixtures in crushed

lord

make me

chaste

but not

yet

---

1 Gimhae is a small town, once isolated and shunned for its population of Indian halfbreeds spawned by the marriage of a Korean king with an Indian princess. Even so, small-town Gimhae was the largest city my father and I had ever lived in.

she likes
him

american
man

comfort in
who he is

american
man

does not act
so strong

american
man

more
sensitive

american
man

more like
woman

american
man

mutton
dressed as
lamb

bottles, the cigarette smokers near the parks, the fried chicken stalls near his house, the waste bins outside his apartment, the roses lining his apartment complex, the soaps in the elevator, the antiseptics in the hallway; how he traveled factoring sense[2] . . .

. . . and it was thus that The FATHER saw in her an expat's warning; never to marry a Korean woman, no access to your own bank account,

> they marry foreign
> men, the men say, so they can
> be the men, men say

that they translate for you, they do everything, which might sound nice until you realize you are the Asian woman, they the white man . . .

. . . for as The FATHER had no Korean license, August drove him up the mountains, to Suriratna's Temple, saying,

> I want to tell you
> I know who you are

---

2 For eight to ten hours a day, my brother, my father, and I all taught English to elementary school students, and for the rest of the day we planned the next day's classes. Large as the city was, we rarely left our main corridor of PC bangs and Chimaek restaurants. Our single street led from our apartment to the hagwan, to the Homeplus Superstore, to the CGV movie theater. I never saw the ancient tombs or took public transit.

and saying thus she guided him up the mountain, through the fish of the gods, and as he got winded up the stairs, August thus said,

> you are god
> descended from heaven

past the monk heads, she spirited The FATHER to Eunhasa, Temple of King Suro, Nimrod the First, saying,

> I know because you
> look just like him

and the lattice flowers adorned the doors to Gwanseeum-bosal, ode to Guanyin, goddess of transition, saying,

> I see god³ in
> your blue eyes

Nimrod who begat Kannon who begat Avalokiteshvara who refused both birth and rebirth and who stayed in this world despite ideations of ending it for the next . . .

my father's
last wish

revamp
transfigure
diverge

no longer
mere dream

where
change

maker
distills

divine
beauty

see your
own

empyrrhical

victory

---

3 My father was fascinated by Korean believers. To them, heaven was a real place, like Ohio. Perhaps it was Ohio. I think he grew jealous of this belief, of a divinity without abstraction. God was not otherworldly, unknowable. God resided in his iris.

ocean's
boundless
poise

...and thus upon a bridge over a pond overlooking Gimhae did August and The FATHER converse until the little red crosses crept up the horizon and into the firmament of stars ...

sky's
lingering
limits, and
no

...and the constellations ministered him, and the jewels in the night sky sparked him ...

more peaks
or summits

...and lo, the stars of her eyes were upon him, as if to crossly question that field of crimson graves.

the gods
they are
they

who hear
the pained
cries of the

multitudes
and stay

LONG GONE DADDY

CHAPTER 7 VERSE 1

f Al Ain,[1] flat city of no inclines or sidewalk gutters to reroute rain; and for The FATHER, no driving, no booze, no women, only worship and work . . .

. . . how safe he felt in the UAE, that idiot-proof country . . .

. . . and to think that The FATHER's FATHER, The Preacher of Restorationist Christianity, was preaching no new movement, just the gulf's exegesis . . .

cast into caste

targeted to become

untarget able

---

1 In October 2009, one month into my PhD program in Seattle, I could no longer stand living in the US (again). I considered leaving to teach at a glorified overseas school (again). My father, well over South Korea by then, sent me an ad:

Job Title: Teacher
Located at: Al Ain, United Arab Emirates (UAE)
Vacancy: 5 or more
Salary: $5718 USD a month

My father got the job, while I chose to stick it out in academia. To this day, I often imagine an alternative me who lives in Al Ain: no PhD, no investment in academic institutions. Like my father, no need to charm a flock.

scour the world for any

. . . lo, and how the gulf knew all the new ways to present power; how so too The FATHER knew his own death throes, knew his kind was nearing extinction . . .

where that can abide scum like

. . . lo, and how the olfactory factory of Al Ain was not the floral scents of the Korean churches, but the earth's musks of clove, jasmine, frankincense, and, finally, ochre . . .

you give yourself to

. . . the faded scent of body odor, harsh at first,[2] but given its ubiquity, The FATHER came to admire it, declaring,

the sea let home become the

not odor

soil you wash up on

but hormonal

aroma

---

2   In 2015, a year and a half after receiving my PhD, I visited Dubai to interview for an academic job. The city reminded me of Las Vegas—desert landscape, gold parlors, brown workers. And, certainly, the money was nothing to sneer at.

Job Title: Assistant Professor
Provision: 15% pay raise per year (mandatory)
Provision: Free of charge furnished housing
Salary: $5717 USD a month (untaxed)

I was offered the job, but declined to live in a place where fornication, drink, and queer love were punishable sins. Never again. Still, an alternative me broils at the me writing this from North America. I imagine him, Dubai me, visiting my father on weekends, the two of us sneaking Jameson into our coffees and flinging our middle fingers at all the suits and tycoons who flock on by.

CHAPTER 7 VERSE 2

nd so The FATHER knew it would take time to feel properly synched to the new holy lands, to stop rubbing the balmy air from his arms, to stroll the gardens of that garden city; Al Ain, say the expats, has the friendliest khaleejis in the world, but,

no
        just
ice

        just
the

        just
us

all i want to know

what is in the medicine

some fresh air to breath

and how The FATHER felt that his presence, to that nest of squalling students, was a running joke, and how The FATHER did manage their behavior until the day they discovered he was a preacher's son, the son of a king maker, and how The FATHER did say unto his charges,

I've always been a
whore   my father my
pimp   cuz you know
cold dead eyes still
try   to pimp me

... and lo, in time their wonderment would wane, for what was Abrahamic royalty doing so far from home? ...

... and those students and teachers and palatial parents all thinking, how badly did he cold cock it all up? ...

believe the poets

... or, are all those cold cocks The FATHER escaped ...

when they say that the day is

... still awaiting his return[1] ...

vibrant with love but

the night is also alive

---

1   By the time my father was in Al Ain, he had taught middle school in Portland, Las Vegas, and three different Korean cities. As a vocal Campbellist, silent Jungian, and budding Peterson stan, he could not help comparing his students' coming-of-age tales. He told me about a boy from Yemen who chased the other children with his shoe, threatening to pound their backsides. My father believed the Yemeni children shared something with the brown children in Portland, and the Black children in Las Vegas, and the darker-skinned, curly-haired children in South Korea. Wherever my father taught, he gave these students special attention, talked them through their meltdowns, and blamed bullying on the lighter-skinned bullies. Perhaps he saw us in them, his own bullied brown boys. Perhaps an alternative me would have lit up to have a teacher like my father at an 8 a.m. roll call.

nd yea still every time The FATHER visited that british coffee chain in Al Ain's
Al Ain mall, the chats between himself
and The Future Wife[2] grew more and
more familiar; he who hadn't been to the Philippines for
more than a stint could yet read her body language, her
sensual gloam; how the first time she sidled up beside
him after he sugared his Americano and he thought of that
line, she makes me want to be a better . . .

they[1] left

me

abandoned

me

wholesale

> glad you could
>
> make it
>
> lovesome

the

I need to go to

the gym more

yin

no, I don't

mind your gut

his

. . . and how just beneath the table but fully in his view
The Future Wife placed her eyelash strips upon her bare
knee and knock-knocked his denim-shielded thigh; lo,
came a small bout of wind; low, where that dress rustled;

yen

for

hems

---

1 By the time my father moved to Al Ain, my brother, my sister, my
mother, and I had all severed ties with him.

2 My father met his second wife in Al Ain. Within a year, he went
from searching for open skies to bunking in like a hermit.

high, where a blush flitted across her face and she spoke
thus about a lazy server,

future wife
girl from

the café girl
half his age

girl from
billiran

wait	some people
your favorite	just need to be slapped
color is	around
sunrise?	a little

saith The Future Wife, the Emirates treat the Filipinos like
animals; Dad-joketh The FATHER, yes but here tiger paws
claw into leather backseats and hospitals are built for fal-
cons, so the Emirates treat animals pretty well; snarkithly
replied The Future Wife, you mean their Filipino workers
treat them well . . .

. . . and how The FATHER would need her when his gout
came, those old twining nerve endings grasping in full-
throated screams so absurdly hurtful; how she would
help him unload those loud keening yawps, the incoher-
ent moans . . .

danny	do not eat the blue
	berry muffin
	left out too long it's
	perish
parish	able

---

3 My father was enamored with her love for God and God's wor-
shippers. He went on binges, she saw his better side. Perhaps he
wanted to believe in his own redemption, too.

. . . thinking, who the fuck is she; I'm fucking starving[4] . . .

. . . and The Future Wife could not know that something so small had the capacity to set him off[5] . . .

. . . for now was The FATHER miraculously on the wagon,[6] but . . .

exalt and

. . . for the first time in months, felt that itch to be perishable,[7]

billow cheap

sake sage

               you're not yourself

in   father sick

shall   days away it seems from

ah

---

4 I've often wondered if my father's body image was as mangled up as my own. Going from fat to normie in my teens was determined by a very intentional but very slow process of wishy-washy anorexia and banal bulimia. I once starved myself for five days straight until my tongue lashed at my teeth as if they were sustenance. I spat out food into napkins of tall nimbus clouds. Growing up, anorexia was like queerness was like suicidal thoughts: they all seemed to go together. And I believed everyone was just in the closet about all of them.

5 This is all to say: Aphrodite, do fathers pass this on to their sons?

6 Or, do I mean to say: Anorexie, please keep our faces from revealing the shame we feel for our bodies.

7 so that our sons never see it.

happiness is
be

ing under one
hundred and

sixty pounds
mama

bang

bang

shoot

shoot

... and how it all made sense here in the new holy lands;
God and the help and the helplessness here belonged in
the same breath ...

*these
katulong—
"help*

... here where words were a consoling embrace to share,
to help ...

*ers," as we
called
them—were
oft*

... to not wither away alone[8] ...

*en younger
but al*

*ways aging
faster ... their
lungs*

*fried by
bleach and
pet*

*roleum
vapors*

---

dust choked

*and light
years from
home*

we roam

8 My father and I both caught the travel bug at the same time. Together we cruised through Japan, Malaysia, and the Korean penin-
sula. After a decade of travel, he had amassed dozens of close calls:
being beaten by a mob in Busan, getting kidnapped in Oman, nar-
rowly avoiding a market bomb in Egypt during the Arab Spring. His
travel stories were always a mixture of proclaiming his own bravery
and a thinly disguised call for help.

CHAPTER 7 VERSE 4

T hen did The FATHER roam past the bed-
ouin arches and past his casted shadow
and past the rotating fountain beams . . .

. . . past the potted palm fronds of the
holy hilton lobby and past the bollywood flash mob live
instagram recordings and past the tex mex bar and into
the wild night where he felt solace sitting alone with that
friendly taste; the club entrance, that segregated gateway
into mayhem . . .

. . . and how The FATHER skulked inside amongst the
barstools, upended his first whiskey coke and gingerly set
his weight upon his injured toe . . .

. . . and yea did he pump hands with a clan of Emirates,
thinking, how they pass down positions, horse-trade up,[1]
and are they rich rich? Sure, but as they say, they care more
about ego than profit margins than the marginalized . . .

the first to circum

locute the globe, how his boys

deplore the lord and

his unpardon able sin

---

1 My father often complained about the way Filipinos were treated
in the UAE. And Indians. And Pakistanis. And Yemenis. He believed 9/11 was a hoax and the war on terror was a light show and
got all his news from Facebook. But in a way even his conspiracy
theories were just attempts to understand the bidding wars all
around him.

... and The FATHER asked unto the young men dressed head-to-toe in white crease-free kanduras what they thought of labor camps; laughing and drunk themselves, one traded a bracelet for The FATHER's baseball cap, another tapped him, finger jab, into the crown of his head, and saith to him thus,

> free speech is like bummed
> cigarettes, always on loan
> and bad for your health

drunken
slurs

forecast half
gestated

that hath The FATHER thinking, you emirates got hotels for everything, you go to Aloft for Asians, the Radisson for Russians, come get your escort of choice ...

organ
drones

... and how in The FATHER's soused-up mind did he hear that gouty toe saith to him thus,

> your lad[2]
> piped paeans to peoples gone mad
> your shoes
> dusted in desert filtered gold
>
> your mouth[3]

---

2 I separated myself from my father for years. I needed help pivoting.

3 I longed to be from a different family, for a different story of where I'm from, to pretend-away the deserted father.

broke brazen broadcasts
your lungs
fired charred cannonballs

free sky
shades

your bald spot
dissolving city square

slide over
the ruins

your baby blue eyes
thirst to an unearthed well[4]

of mankind

your race[5]
spot spores of bread mold
your throat
coarse ditch about to croak

your mind
doused dark mine
your skin[6]
cockroach pissed scared

and upon the toe saying thus, the three young men gave
The FATHER a comrade bump on the shoulder, saying,

---

4 Academia gave me a different approach to the problem, a way to channel the guilt deep within me.

5 My immigrant families, my brown lineage. For the first time I was no longer encouraged to hide or throw away the family Guillermo.

6 And in the academy, white papas are the first to face Lady Guillotine.

come and finish your
drink and join us just outside
we'll go for a drive

and how The FATHER, slurping from his glass like a
pooch dying of thirst, did get in the car . . .

s it was among the car's musty scent of tobacco and hormonal aroma and as it was behind the windows of desert rushing at one hundred sixty kilometers an hour and as it was within the whiskey-drenched cinematography of jeweled beams encircled by lights blurred in honey red, The FATHER did teach his new disciples, who set upon him with their camera phones saying, meet my American friend! Hey, friend, say something funny again! And The FATHER opened his mouth to say,

> I love all people
> bronze azure amber
> enameled wood

flinch

sucking in

sharp breath

teeth shivs

twitch

and their laughter made The FATHER glad to entertain them, for wasn't this pedagogy? Thinking, laughter and play; I do appreciate this about the Emirates, so touchy, hand in hand, one still wearing The FATHER's hat, saying,

> my wife cannot
> how can she say the quran says
> if she just reads it in her own way
>
> not whether I agree with
> it's whether the authorities

I cannot warn her enough

sand-
smeared sky

all alight,

all ablaze,

o where are
my

american
stars?

and The FATHER saw that they were passing the graves of dead foreign workers whose families could not afford to send their bodies home; how The FATHER had been warned that the desert eats cars and strands tourists, and thus he knew they were taking him to Jebel Hafeet,

Where we go? Let me guess. We go to Oh man. Oh ma ma. Oh man.

Oh man! Oh ma ma! Oh man!

and out of the car The FATHER felt that barely discernible wobbly leg, heard the susurrations and giggles, thinking, well these guys aren't russians and well I haven't talked to any local women so no way they'd kill me; and it wasn't that The FATHER was afraid of death anyways just that injuries grew more permanent with age and he didn't need more than the daily feeling of desert cold singeing his gouty toe . . .

. . . Oman on one side, UAE on the other, at cross Sultanates where the disciples did alight that fire pit into a wild dazzling flame . . .

. . . and yea did The FATHER share a San Miguel, saying this is not from Mexico, and in a burst of song did he unfurl that blessed voice . . .

a dog that's been beat
too much
spend half your life just
coverin' up

and yea did The FATHER look deeper into that fire pit
of gravel and yea did the fire bless him with a vision of
blessed young men among soju and samgyupsal, saying
near the desert fire,

chingu chingu chingu
no no no me ajashi

*you've
stabbed me
enough*

and how hollers did tear from his lungs, the voices
drowned by gusts of wind and blotches of moonlight un-
veiling the canyon's weathered red rock; and yea did The
FATHER see them too within the fire, The blessed dark
desert Sons drawing faces in the sand, comic panels and
word clouds, saying,

*you can go
now*

why does the wind
tug at the cloud
stretching it too thin in directions
it does not care to go?

and yea as The FATHER felt the howling maelstrom did
the boys transform into girls; The blessed Mother giving
milk to the infant girl's sagged head . . .

...and how as breath drew out of him The FATHER thereupon decided to do it all again, to give her, the new her, a shiny rock harvested from the guts of the earth by a child at gunpoint ...

...and yea at four-twelve in the morning did The FATHER feel himself submerged and yea did he hear his brother's voice through the ripples, and yea as he saw the cape side tenements did he finally feel merged, thus saying,

look danny
I'm in

the desert
but I'm not
lost

look how far
I've come

I've kept on in the
world, danny, but the nimrod
the nimrod still stares

still stares at me from
the coast with that silence that
silence of ourselves

that threatens that
threatens to recompose

don't say a
word, no

just come
and rise
with me, sun

rival
everyone

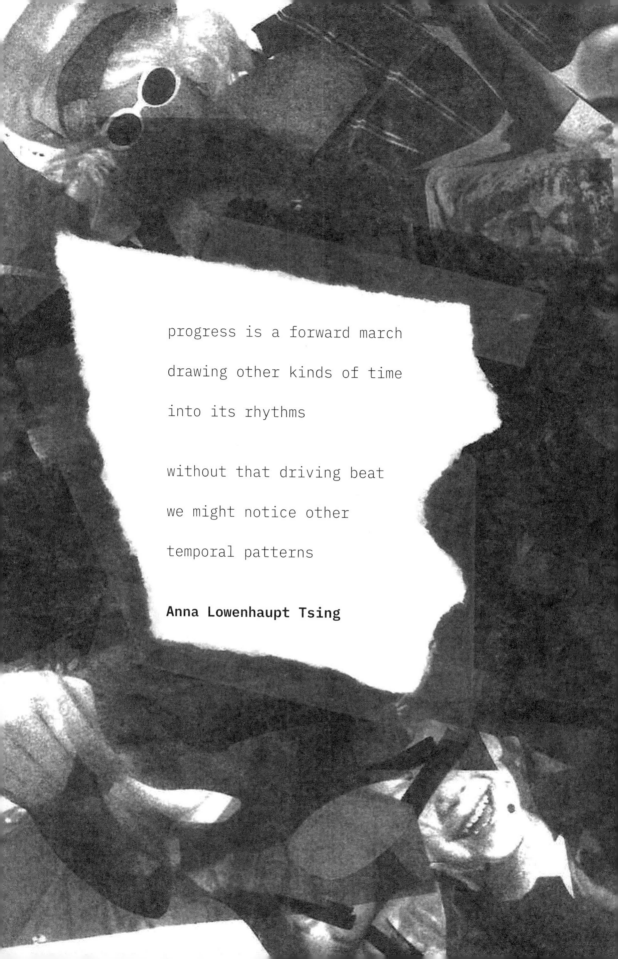

progress is a forward march

drawing other kinds of time

into its rhythms

without that driving beat

we might notice other

temporal patterns

Anna Lowenhaupt Tsing

epode

three / card / digression

SISSY / SISTER / CIS

I sing a
madcap
song
of what
life could
even be
without
the
restless
feelings
and the
wreckless
thoughts
and the
starveling
love
that
simply
needs
a wild
wild
dream

cords of interlaced wire
speak
theories of the mesh

grafting branches
spore
fruity scion stocks

energized circuits
spark
friction tribble touch

echoes in re-verbs

minor chords in D

revolt

archepeggio

reveal

refuse

refurbish

revoke

repulse

record

reclaim

recoil

recon

revolve

revive

relate

relinquish

revenge

remove

remain

resent

this is my guitar speaking
in strummed songs
        of hollow wood and steel bridges
            that spill air into climate into wind into
                            breath

            snowy hill   dirt skin
    our cold space
                struck

x
x
x
x
x

they say the music you listen to at thirteen is what you'll
be listening to for the rest of your life   I was thirteen in
1997 when NIMROD. was released

other
wise
a
wise
other

a metalhead on the church bus told me to buy the album during
a youth group retreat   "it's fake punk but good"   I listened and
felt seized   the violin intro of hitchin' a ride   the instrumental of
last ride in   the nonsense of jinx crossdressing at the age of four
billie joe bj chaplin tramp in purple dress stunning fake punk
I learned to play every song on my nylon guitar   I longed to make
music that could seize

she allows herself
caught in their threading
anonymously in their thick
motion in the weight of
their utterance

I wrote songs developed a voice of slurs
and screeches and started a band it
never occurred to me that I could be the
lead that I could be punk

burned
out
&
out
strung

now I hear the minors   I hear how the songs were written
just after the birth of a son to a man who had no map for
fatherhood   no threads to tune

punk made   me a   mutt a

mango   mongol   mongrel

I was somewhere around

sissy   sister   cis

I don't feel like a man
        or a woman. I feel like
                shit.

genesis of   genre fluid   gender bender

femininity . . .
        has become a
            disappearing
            horizon

sex drained   sick stranged   six stringed

the world was
        turning over my mother
                        was crying

peaks on a
horizon   ash clouds the
                other   to distant boats
                                adrift

        all   look   blurred

Starting at the age of seven I began to talk-story with my brother every night imagining we were video game characters animals plants and bombs

my name the first act of de prived consent

Starting at the age of eleven we shifted to chat-room roleplaying on a computer near my parents' room where I could hear them throwing loose change

clandestine
operations
break
reality's
looms

Starting at the age of fifteen I hung with a crowd of punk rock girls whose red plaid skirts were my armor against the red-laced skinheads we played with make up and making ourselves up

priapic
heads
snapping
addled on
adrenaline
lost to the
plunge

Starting at the age of nineteen I hitched a ride and then hopped around Asia for a decade slimming myself to the size of my backpack

Kawika the one with the mole just below the chin
so it always looks like a raindrop is about to form or tear

It tastes good and it's like moisturizer
said SOPHIE on why SOPHIE chose SOPHIE's name before SOPHIE
died in Greece while trying to take a picture of the moon

every bad thing
that threatens people I love;
for me, dread only

                                          I never felt gender dysphoria never
                                          felt that my true self was man or
            narcissism   woman or nonbinary of any type
                vanity   just knew I didn't love myself or like
            selfishness   myself or want to be inside my body
              sure—but   for various reasons and sometimes
            never   pride   escaping my place in society was less
                                          about escaping my gender but just
                                          escaping the place, that is escaping
    travel changes you   the society which held me to a
        as you move through this place
    and this world you change
        in return life—and travel—leaves marks on you

I get why he did it   that's enlightenment enough to know that
    even with that zest for   there is no final resting place of the
      people for pleasure for   mind no moment of smug
              taste for   clarity

                    bright days but   *I may stop knowing*
                    darker nights   *how to like and desire*
                                             the world around me

I'm living in Hong Kong in 2017 when the
copyedits come in for my first book
the copyedit   mythical pristine fountain
of youth   they can't stop you now

my partner goes silent as I read her the acknowledgments
why   didn't   you   include   your   father
since life without him   life has only brightened
in interviews I do not mention him or *that side*

I put myself out there   knowing the white puritan anti-
vaxxers won't bother looking me up or reading a word of my work

light-skinned prof   ethnic penname   biracial punk penning tracts
against identity in Hong Kong surrounded by all these Europeans

my father teaches at a Catholic school   I teach above a cathedral
we can cooperate with our enemies but not each   other

an American grouch sitting on the 68th floor of
a high-rise writing on Marx and the multitudes

my son is born in Hong Kong and they
say tear gas can kill a one-year-old

the third draft of copyedits   the final
final draft   I break and toss his name in
buried in a paragraph I'd like to thank my
peers   and   Samuel   James   Patterson

me or some how
time   builds   up
th   owe
  e   d

thought is elliptical
it tracks concepts and allows for
unfinishedness inducing
itself to become misshapen

OMG… did you know
you can't even find
Trump's / the US
government's official
website. Try it.. Hahaha
you say. Did you know
you have been bullying
and stripping Americans
from there rights..
Hahaha.. you don't care.
[…] You do know you
lost right? You do know
the other party lost and
were not downright
satanic about it right?
Grow up idiots. We are
tired of you.

for

a decade

we

spoke

only through

text

he

wrote only

in

ellipses

I/We, want to
meet up with
you guys.
Problem is ..
mostly money,
haha. True. […]
I hope you
don't think my
dna is evil…I
know your
research and
Chris.. We are
not our
parents, or
grandparents,
or great
grandparents..
I hope you agree.

I lived in Asia
and

love Asia just so that you know. Sorry about the skin color. I
know it is a problem for you. .I hopw you are Okay
Sorry for it's lightness that is..
If I could make it darker, I would

I'm not
intimidated
by you.

I don't care
that you
have a ph.d.

no one gives
a mouse's
patootie
about history
of a whitie.

Haha . we
are the
privileged.

But I can't
figure when I
knew
privilege or
how to use
it.

he..

wrote..

as..

his..

thoughts..

elapsed..

..

words..

always..

were..

elliptical..

I challenge my
sons.. I \m sorry
to challenge you..
I was challenged..
Its like a tradition
in my family....

Here is the thing
Chris...U
will find a conflict or a
righteous fight, where you
might just say .. your life is
ok to give for this fight..
00s ok as a martar. . il

Ellipses might be a figure of loss or plenitude: Sometimes it is more efficient to go dot dot dot. Sometimes it's also a way of signaling an elision. Sometimes the referent is beyond words.

my white grandfather wrote twelve educational books on christianity   I still keep his last book on my shelf *Search for True Discipleship in Church History*

Supreme, sovereign, infinite deity planned it from the beginning: a teaching/discipling church—a Growing Christian Teaching/Discipling Church.

octopedal   church moist consentacled church   growing erecting disciplining church

I awry his funeral strive to bring peace plan an epode

In a world gone awry since the Garden of Eden God has striven to bring to all mankind his saving plan.

The most highly skilled, intensive care available must be provided if the suffering patient is to survive.

before he went into intensive care that highly demented man did not recognize me but when he looked at me he talked about how he saw a lot of asian whores during the war but did not see their suffering or what else those folks did to survive

the ode the Lord's pants falling saying to his wife   oh just let them fall   no cure with each step pants searching down stain boxers didn't care

We owe it to ourselves, as well as to our Lord, to search and find the best possible care and cure

and to see that it is administered before it is too late.

nothing ministered against women gays us he gives me none of this he hated the pulpit believed in small communities working things out before it is too late perhaps his glares were just meant to see

x
x
x
x
x

when my novel stamped won the asian american
studies book award I would have stood up and turned
my back against me if not for covid if not for it already
being a punk hate anthem not so much anti-travel just
anti-me

exaggerated
a fucked up kind of
feminine

he could have gone all the way,
but he shuddered at the thought
of being trapped in a woman's
body

inherited my
father's
broad shoulders
and chia-pet
arms

and   just   how   many
brown   trans   girl
professors do you know?

He stared at that mascara-ridden
face in the mirror. Blurry
vision saw nothing wrong. He
saw himself, still, his mother's
offspring.

she still saw her mother's
son

but is there anything more
pleasing to the white gays than
a once-domineering
asian man
turned smiley skinny
emo   e   fem
boi

I had a student with long corn colored hair   a popcorn throwing charmer   who went by he or she or they and she he or they once said how annoyed they he or she feels when she they or he gets called courageous   that sometimes he she or they feels that this word courage is just a seed of what someone is really trying to say   whether they he or she   that you have the courage to do what I am just too weak and too afraid to do   my last words to them her and him just before summer broke as he she or they were handing in their final paper were you have   so   so   so   much courage.

×
×
×
×
×
×

TRACK 2

RE / CON / SILE

fuck you and I love you and fuck you and I love you and fuck you and I
love you and fuck you and I love you and fuck you and I love you and fuck

you and I love you
and fuck you and I
love you and fuck
you and I love you
and fuck you and I
love you and fuck
you and I love you
and fuck you and I
love you and fuck
you and I love you
and fuck you and I
love you and fuck
you and I love you
and fuck you and I
love you and fuck
you and I love you
and fuck you and I
love you and fuck
you and I love you
and fuck you and I
love you and fuck
you and I love you
and fuck you and I

love you and fuck you and I love you and fuck you and I love you and fuck
you and I love you and fuck you and I love you and fuck you and I love

dear son

it's november
2018 and you're
fifteen months old
still not
walking when you
have your first
seizure

I'm on a return
layover in chicago
when I get the
call

your mother
rushes you to the
hospital

her words on the
text are
unintelligible

in six hours I'm
there

Dear Dad,

It's July 2018 and I've just moved to Vancouver with my wife and your grandson after five years of living in China and Hong Kong. For the first time in a long time, I live within close proximity to you. After a decade abroad, you've moved back to Portland to help care for Grandma. Until now, you've never met my wife or my son. You never visited me in Nanjing or Hong Kong (I'm not holding it against you, no one did). You would have come to our wedding in Canada, you say, but there was some flimsy rule about crossing national borders with a DUI.

Before you arrive, we hide the alcohol in our closet. We think you might get drunk around my son. Or maybe you will get righteous and teach him about God. To me, this is just as frightening.

You come by bus. I show up in an expensive suit, you in an Oregon salmon-fishing T-shirt. I look like a dandy, and well you're white—an expense that cannot be taken off.

after five days in
the hospital we
have no clue what's
wrong with you

the mystery of your
sickness gnaws at
us for two months
until it happens
again and this time
I am there

I call 911 and the
firemen threaten to
kick down the door

medics come

police come

in the ambulance
your eyelids
twitch

You haven't changed since I last saw you. During
dinner your cracked phone shows us a video of
Morgan Freeman saying that there should be
no Black history month. I disagree with Morgan
Freeman. You keep pushing. I tell you I'm allowed
to disagree with a Black guy who gets paid to play
god on TV.

I spend the next day trying to keep my eye on you.
When I leave to teach a class, I lose you. I call and
call and an hour passes. When I find you touring
University Way, I smell your familiar booze-
breath. By the way you walk, the way you talk,
I can tell. You're only a couple of beers in.

I take you on a detour of the college campus until
you're sober enough to be around my son. At the
Reconciliation Pole, I tell you about the thousands
of Indigenous children who died in Canada's
residential schools, represented by over 68,000
copper nails hammered onto the Pole by survivors
and their families.

Tears form in your eyes. Why, you ask, would
they even seek reconciliation? They should call
it the genocide pole.

five days more
in hospital and
they tell us

you have a rare
genetic
syndrome

only one in
60,000 kids has
it

there isn't a lot
of data

no help groups

no guides

some don't
survive

and this

disease it
comes

from his
father's

genes

At dinner you tell me that you're no longer a teacher. For now, you have a job at an Amazon warehouse, processing and fulfilling orders. The company didn't even ask for a CV, and the hours are long, and the pay is crap. But you call it a welcomed break. You make a dad joke: "After twenty years of teaching children, this new job fulfilling Amazon orders won't be quite as fulfilling." I actually laugh.

I tell you I'm finishing my manuscript—copyedits for my second academic book about information technology and the low-wage factory work of debt slaves in China. It's about how we have such a difficult time feeling compassion for those who are an ocean away, who don't look or talk like us. This time, you laugh.

Something warm exudes from you
Something I only saw as the calm before the storm

We eat. There's no alcohol, no nearby bars. For now, you are here with us, present. You bring up Duterte and we argue but then we have dessert and we're OK. We play with my son. You try to hug him and he lets you.

"Appreciate that while you can," you say.

it's not courage that keeps you
hanging on, just a pessimism

that has earned your trust
of who you are and

what happens next

Two months after your visit and one month after my son's first hospital stay, I get an email from your sister, who is living with you in Portland.

She says that you were taking care of Grandma and there was an incident. Grandma fell down the stairs and broke her hip. She says that the police came and that you attacked them, perhaps too drunk to know what you were doing. You are now in jail.

Later, my aunt elaborates. You had blood all over your shirt. You were screaming, in a rage. One might say you ran amok, or went full gangster thug. But no. You are Baby Blue, so you were just going through a hard day. You get released the next morning.

I give my best wishes to my aunt.

six months of
horrorshow

taking your
blood sugar

seducing you to
eat

losing teeth

to weakened
enamel

we get you on
hormones

you heal, you
grow

we give you
whatever you
want

x
x x
x x
x

During my son's second hospital stay in January 2019, I get another email from your sister. She says that you tried to commit suicide. Again. She won't say how, or what state you were found in. And I don't ask.

I'm told that you left a suicide note, addressed to the family, and to me. I know if I push hard enough, I can get my aunt to show me the note. I could see the words that you would only share with me after death.

I don't push.

you get used to
it

I see you
staring off into

space I watch
you play with
numbers

and letters
while the world
stays out

of your way
playing

games in your
head

baby blue

golden brown

my love

how will life

color you?

the worse things got for you the
more you provoked our hate

the only logic I could see was
you didn't want us to miss you

when you finally decided to leave

x
x
x
x
x
x

As my son's health begins to recover, I invite you to visit again. This time, before we have dinner, before I lose you at the nearest bar, I try to clear the air.

Do you realize we're the same age that Dad was when his brother died?

I ask you about the suicide attempt, but you do not answer. You've never been able to talk about your problems. Your alcoholism, your dead brother, your rage. But of this, I want to know. I need to know.

I get wanting to destroy yourself, not wanting to see tomorrow. But I don't understand *your* longing for death. I was an unwanted birth, a statistical exemption to the IUD that mom didn't realize was two hapa twins away from being foolproof. For this and other reasons, my own death always felt just, a means of rebalancing the universe by getting rid of its most libido-driven scion.

Wtf

OK bro

Yeah that . . .

hmm

I mean I think I get why he ruined his life

But your birth was no accident. You were loved and you loved your parents. You were welcomed by your community. You had siblings, uncles, aunts, who loved you. You had whiteness, maleness, good looks, strength, health, a religion where people like you could go abroad and be seen as gods. You had everything, Baby Blue Eyes.

Dude I texted him.

I think about all this while I'm sitting across from you at a Tim Horton's, waiting for your bus to take you back to Portland. I want to tell you I'm sorry, though I'm not. I want to ask you what was in your suicide note, though I don't want to know. Sometimes reconciliation is just a con, and no amount of armchair thinking can materialize forgiveness.

That's fucking awful thinking of that if that happened now I don't know how I would survive it.

The bus comes and you stand to leave and something inside me pulls me to hug you. You're large, and my arms can't fit all the way, so I just link my fingers. You feel cold, frozen in time.

There's no way I feel to overstate that.

"Thank you," you say. I know why you say it. You think I'm just waiting for you to leave because we're all better off without you. I know you think this because these thoughts are not strangers to me.

I don't know how I would survive it.

So I hug you again, harder. You might be right. Maybe I don't mean it. But I feel something might grow out of the warmth created by two bodies pressed together.

reconciliation starts with the stories
of what you did to them

it's a swaying, teetering line
but you must walk it

it's the bridge they've built
for you to cross

ME / MORE / IRE

The Revolution starts here + now within each one us.

Burn down the walls that say you can't:

Be a dork, tell your friends you love them.

Resist the temptation to veiw those around you as objects + use them.

Recognize empathy and vulnerability as positive forms of strength.

Resist the internalization of capitalism, the reducing of people + oneself to commodities meant to be consumed.

Resist psychic death.

Don't allow the world to make you into a bitter abusive asshole.

Cry in public.

Don't judge other people. Learn to love yourself.

Acknowledge emotional violence as real.

Figure out how the idea of competition (winning and losing) fits into your intimate relationships.

Decide that you'd rather be happy than be right all the time.

Believe people when they tell you they are hurting or are in pain.

Trust.

I ride   I write   I writhe

in my head but not alone

writing is fighting said ishmael reed
or was it frank chin?

                                              what if language

solmaz sharif says
the poet is a
caretaker   did not need
      of
            language
 poets mother language   an expert's
care
      listen
              handle   protection?
        let language grow
                touch

                                    connect
                                      mourn

against the fathers'
empowerment   hippocratic oath
empire

                             for writers first
        let it
            matter   be not a
            what we call
humans   hypocrite
        bodies
             selves

                          you   I   and us

moving to Vancouver was my second biggest lesson in patience, after
fathering a child

skies dampen

spirit   sensation   intellect

evil is in the trivial
            and we are
                    devils of boredom

gray   drops   slip   past   your   knuckles

cringe racism   watered down racism   lulu racism

tears never
fall
            from my eyes

false   creek   fluids   slither   through   false   city

bottom-shelf racism   under-the-table racism   over-prescribed racism

but in the
rain I drop
into grief

tfw you're taking out the recycling thinking man another day of crazy
party drinking just look at all these liquor bottles then realizing you
haven't had a party in months because it's covid and the only partier in
the house during that time has been you

cherry blossoms

treat: read: queer:

                                                  exotic asia

                    all flowers
                      made
                    to bloom

open color in full sunny bright
        close off in deadening white
        wilt and get cast
                into trash

                    This is fascism.
                      Dinner party
                    by dinner party

                            and what tastes better
                                than a buffet of color

when you think of us think

of coming once a year
        reflecting sunset and causing accidents
                tossing off and sporing petals
                    all over the place

All,

I'm sorry if my earlier email appeared to be casting blame. I remember our conversations about the difficulties this term and recognize that we're at max in terms of labor and speed.

Chris,

Thank you for your apology. I did receive your email about ███████ committee work as a bit aggressive and blaming. So I appreciate your self-reflection. Under very difficult conditions of the pandemic, we are indeed all working at 'max', as you say. I believe it is my job ██████████ to always try to lift each other up.

Hi ██████████

~~I want to re-post the exact email I sent out below, because from what I make of it there is not a hint of aggression or blaming. As a man of color I am very aware that anything I say or write can come off as aggressive even when there is no intention behind it or any recognizable tonal difference. I'm sure you're familiar with how casting men of color as aggressive is part of structural racism and the ever-expanding carceral system, so I don't have to reiterate that, and how asking them to "self-reflect" and "apologize" for aggression that did not occur can also feed into these systems. As you know I respect you immensely for your research, skill, and commitments, and I also hesitated in saying anything because I don't want to invalidate your feelings if you did feel that I was being dismissive of the gargantuan amount of work that you've been doing (and because this is a very stressful time for everyone). But this has been an ongoing issue since I came to~~ ██████████ ~~and I think increased awareness would really help.~~

I never planned to get a phd or
to become a professor of any kind

I applied to graduate school because, as the rabbit said, why not   I
thought maybe with a master's I could teach in some foreign country
and travel around   it took me three years to get an acceptance despite
having near perfect grades   despite graduating college at nineteen   for
the years in between   I traveled   I taught   I wrote stories and poems   I
rewrote my application essay about james joyce

In 2007 I was accepted to the university of washington's english
program   but was offered no scholarships or funding   I went into
massive debt   my supervisor told me I was only accepted because of my
persistence not my work

acceptance

                 he said I never should   your writing

without   have gotten in   abysmal

                   to grad school

means   your thinking

                 so I routed myself   inferior

is no   through different roots

                         why won't you go

                            away

acceptance

I never planned to get a phd or to become a professor of any kind

but when it comes to vengeance
I am persistent

it's a long time coming
what with our
donors
patrons
nations

so

we have to help ~~assimilate~~ her
~~domesticate~~ her
~~acculturate~~ her
socialize her
to our department

without taking away her
~~fire~~
~~light~~
~~life~~
you know

███████ is
this
████████
how
██
they
████
talked
████
about
████
me ?

    how do we harness ███'s
      flame   into
        flash   into
      flesh

    the em-dash my em—otion
      the redaction my red act██
        the strikethrough ~~strikes~~ the match
        and the grays flash rays
          of
    ~~fire~~—███—light—███—~~life~~

m   y
university
orbits the death star on its least
affordable   moon   in   endor
colonized   Cambodian-like   forests
whose   peoples   turned   stuffed   toys   on
shelves,   oil   rich   trigger   the   blue   blood   rich
camouflaged   in $300   sandals   wealth   appears
poor   educated   share   warnings   of   the   regressive
dumb   some   are   granted   cultural   capital   but
can't   pay   the   rent   and   must   light
fires   to   keep   warm   tell   them   to   write   your   life
but   not   if   your   life   offends   us   nation   of   good
cops   to   America's   bad   cops   the   factual   cop   who
gets   shocked   when   the   other   cop   beats   you   in   your
face   too   shocked   to   pick   up   a   phone   or
a   fist   so   if   all   cops   are   bastards
then   we   cannot
attack   the
death   star   until   the   land   of   endor   first   incites   in   our
l   u   m   i   n   e   s   c   e   n   c   e

me   more   ire

pushed to write   *an auto*   seas of words
about my   *biography*   crafts
self   *gestures to*   we build to
this is it   *the world of*   carry us
the bipoc   *a reading*   from shelf to
biopic   *self*   shelf

        tidal

                      tattle

                                      tirade

I can't think about those times my mother texts to the family chat
        are you a memoirist
                Yeah it's really hard to remember anything or think about it
            or just a pervert
                        Yeah . . . so let's not!!!

        writer's dilemma: stretch the truth or turn the knife

        interior   infernal   inferior

ground
                                        I draw lines in the
                              sand   with found
swells   sticks
                                        please   don't mix
under   up   sand
writer   for stone

I know nothing of craft

I know only the industrial sewer

    how to read its maps

        how to direct its channels of waste

from wreckage to reservoir

    toxic yet full of color

a scavenger for salvage

    I am drawn to the scents of the piled

                up patch

academy   refuse   home

Dear counselors and therapeutics,

In answer to your question, "Are you still having suicidal thoughts?"

Noooo . . . . . ?

Heh . . . why . . . of course . . . not . . .

Not really, but I've been tugging on its roots.

Not really, but I'm still thinking of ways to provoke some hero's gun.

Not really, but if I was crossing the street and a car came barreling toward me, I'm not sure I'd get out of the way.

Not really, but if I lost everything and turned into my father I'd still feel the same.

Not really, but is it high-risk behavior to testify to one's own faithless yearnings—for the pleasure of pleasing, the desire to be desired—and trust a jury of readers not to convict?

Not really, but I still tend to keep myself on the hook. For example, this book.

Not really
but I still fight
like I am

Not really
but I still write
like I am

Can you ever forgive and forget?   (from a conversation in the
Yes   overwatch general textbox while
You can certainly forgive   waiting for the next game to start)

I wanted to publish this book after you died.
It felt like your death could happen any minute.

                                              and then I changed
                                                    my mind

I feared we might lose you.
And your troubled life would be confined
into abstraction.

                              you taught me to protect myself
                  by telling the racist bullies I was mostly white
                    but academe taught me to do the opposite

I sought to sever ties with you, again and again.

                          your whiteness made that easier to do

I thought you were going to die when I started writing this.

                              a good person might have waited

A good person would have.

                                  but I can make you an offer
                                    a deal between patriarchs

I'll forget everything, if you forgive me for this.

ENVOI

42   Mashuq Mushtaq Deen, from my interview with him on *The JAAS Podcast*, in the first two italicized paragraphs.

44   ContraPoints, "that must be super fucking hard for you," a common line from her YouTube channel.

44   Thank you to Danielle Wong for helping work through this poem.

45   Thank you to the Patterson family.

52   Eunsong Kim, in italics.

56   Gayatri Spivak, in italics. Her context is the partition of India and Pakistan.

57   Thank you, Josh Jenkins, for seeing me through these moments.

58   James Baldwin, *Notes of a Native Son*, in italics.

61   Eve Sedgwick, *A Dialogue on Love*, 7, in italics.

62   Thank you, Christine Kim, for helping work through this and other poems.

64   ContraPoints, "Archives: Gender Dysphoria," in italics.

66   Eve Sedgwick, *A Dialogue on Love*, 18, first italics.

66   The second italics are a play on Louise Glück's poem "Faithful and Virtuous Night."

66   Mahalo nui to my cousin, Kamalona Dickens, who took his own life as this book was being written. I'll see you on that other shore.

71   谢谢 to my friends and colleagues in Nanjing, China, for your laughter and your secrets.

72   Kanye West, "I tried to tell you but all I could say."

72   Mitski, "I work better under a deadline."

73   Thank you to my late mentor and friend Donald Goellnicht, who refused to hide the contradictions of our academic realities.

73   Thank you to my in-laws, Heung and Yok Troeung, for your support and care, and for always being there.

73   Pearl Jam, "hope could grow from dirt like me."

76–85   Green Day, "Dickhead fuckface cocksmoking motherfucking asshole waste of semen I hope you," from the song "Platypus (I Hate You)."

87   Laura Marks (in italics), quoted in Nguyen Tan Hoang.

87   Thank you, Larissa Lai, for your writings that speak to transformative forms.

89   Maraming salamat to Jose Dalisay Jr., R. Zamora Linmark, M. Evelina Galang, Michael Gonzalez, and the many writers within the Filipin/x orbit.

92   Bible, King James Version, Exodus 20:7, "Thou shalt not . . . his name."

92 "depressed in the past . . . present" is a common aphorism, usually (and falsely) attributed to Lao Tzu.

93 Sara Ahmed, "bodies stand out when they are out of place."

93 Bible, KJV, Ephesians 5:20, "for the husband is . . . its savior."

94 From "How Great Thou Art," Bible hymn, in haiku.

94 James Baldwin, *The Fire Next Time*, "the blacks simply . . . the whites."

94 Jimmy Buffett, "some people claim . . . damn fault."

100 Thank you to my uncle, Daniel Durwood Patterson, whose memory animates my life and work.

103 Bible, ISV and KJV, Genesis 10:9, "mighty hunter before the Lord . . . began to be mighty in the earth."

107–8 Thank you to my late grandmother Mary Patterson, whose stories inspired much of my speculative fiction, including these lines from *All Flowers Bloom*: "every generation . . . themselves" (303), and "hands worn . . . to speak" (305).

111 Eve Sedgwick, *A Dialogue on Love*, "the foundation of all . . . existence" (11).

112 Barbara Christian, "what I write and how . . . my own life."

113 Du Fu, "Death certain as life, we advance—" from the poem "Onward across Borders," 20.

118 Audre Lorde, *Zami*, "island women make . . . worse" (9).

121 Jesmyn Ward's *Salvage the Bones*, "my head . . . down" (235).

123 Khosal Khiev from *Cambodian Son* by Sugano Masahiro, in italics.

124 Bible, KJV, Jeremiah 20:8–9, "since I spake . . . daily."

127 Douglas Kearney, "we all just trying to leave a mark."

128 "Can I live?" from Jay-Z's 1996 song of the same name, as well as Saidiya Hartman's *Wayward Lives, Beautiful Experiments*, 21.

130 Green Day, "I have no belief, but I," from the song "Walking Contradiction."

133 Green Day, "but—it's too damn late," from the song "Haushinka."

134 Jesmyn Ward, *Salvage the Bones*, "this is Medea wielding the knife this is Medea cutting" (204).

135 bell hooks, "women and children . . . so that they can live."

141 Thank you to my mother, Dion Guillermo Glenn, whose presence will always elude the permanence of words.

144 Marilyn Chin's poem "Autumn Leaves" points out this phrase from the *Tao Te Ching*, in italics.

147 "Marginalia" comes from Gregory Pardlo's poem of the same name.

157 감사합니다 to my inspirational friends who knew me in Gimhae and Seoul.

157 "lord make me chaste but not yet" is a simplified translation of a line by Saint Augustine, "Give me chastity and restraint, but don't do it just yet."

159 Du Fu, "where changemaker distills divine beauty," from the poem "Gazing at the Sacred Peak," 13.

168 The first haiku is from Mia Alvar's story "Shadow Families."

175 Bruce Springsteen and the E Street Band, "a dog that's . . . coverin' up," from the song "Born in the U.S.A."

175 From the film *Chingu*, "you've stabbed me enough, you can go now."

178 Anna Lowenhaupt Tsing, *Mushroom at the End of the World*.

181 The image displays the rules for the historic punk club 924 Gilman.

183 Theresa Hak Kyung Cha, *Dictee*, in italics.

184 "I don't feel like . . . shit" is a play on a line by ContraPoints, "I look inside myself and ask 'do I feel like a man or a woman?' And the answer is that I feel like shit," in the video "Violence."

184 Audre Lorde, *Zami*, "the world was . . . crying" (19).

184 Amber Jamilla Musser, "femininity, I argue, has become a disappearing horizon."

186 Eve Sedgwick, *A Dialogue on Love*, 4, in italics.

186 The lines "I never felt gender dysphoria . . . to a place" and "narcissism, vanity, selfishness, sure—but never pride," were written while watching ContraPoints videos and playing on her words.

186 Anthony Bourdain, "travel changes you . . . on you" (from *The Nasty Bits*) and "that's enlightenment enough . . . smug clarity" (from *No Reservations*, "Peru").

187 唔該嚟 to the writers and friends who helped make Hong Kong a space of warmth and inspiration: Ann Hazel Danao, Collier Nogues, Anjeline de Dios, Nicholas Wong, John Erni, Tammy Lai-Ming Ho, Elmo Gonzaga, Tan Jia, Dorothy Tse, James Shea, Jason Coe, and Doretta Lau.

188–89 Lauren Berlant, interview with *Artforum*, in italics.

190 Thank you to my grandfather, Bill Patterson, whose book *Search for True Discipleship in Church History* is quoted in the five lines in italics (the first two are from page 1, the last three from page 180).

190 The word "consentacle" is from Naomi Clark's game of the same name.

191 *Against Me!*, in italics, from the song "Paralytic States."

191 Rancid, "Blurry vision saw nothing wrong," from the song "Roots Radical."

191 From my first book, *Stamped: An Anti-travel Novel*, "he could have . . . woman's body" (236), and "he stared at that . . . offspring" (106).

193 Thank you to my father, Samuel James Patterson, and my son, Kai Troeung. Without you both, nothing could be imagined or remembered.

193   Image from an infamous cover of Maximum Rocknroll (MRR), published one
      month after Kurt Cobain's suicide.

194   Thank you, Anamaria Richardson, and all the healthcare workers who have re-
      peatedly saved me and my family.

201–2 Thanks to Cameron Patterson, who dealt with all of this, and the this that won't
      stop dealing with us. His words are shaded in gray.

205   Flyer by Kathleen Hanna of Bikini Kill. Photograph: Fales Library NYU/Feminist
      Press.

205   Thank you to my punky interlocutors, Jan Padios and Tara Fickle, for editing
      and giving feedback on so much of my work. Without friends like you, writing
      would not be the same.

206   Solmaz Sharif, from "A Poetry of Proximity," in italics.

207   Thank you to my colleagues whose many meetings helped me grip Canada's
      uniquely slippery racism: Ayesha S. Chaudhry and Rumee Ahmed, Alifa Bandali,
      Denise Ferreira da Silva, JP Catungal, Minelle Mahtani, Janice Stewart, Kim
      Bain, Justin Alger, Ayasha Guerin and Ulrike Zöllner, Mila Zuo and Will Brown.
      I'm glad we're in it together.

208   Solmaz Sharif, from the poem "Force Visibility," in italics.

210   Thank you to Alys Weinbaum, Chandan Reddy, Francisco Benitez, Gillian
      Harkins, LeiLani Nishime, Vicente Rafael, and the many other mentors who
      made my time at UW enthralling.

212   Thank you to my late partner, editor, best friend, and soulmate, Y-Dang
      Troeung, who died during the copyediting stage of this book. You made every-
      thing possible. To you I owe all that I am and all I ever will become. Y-Dang gave
      me the words in gray.

213   Dionne Brand, in italics.

213   Thank you, Laura Cameron, Courtney Berger, and all the editors who saw some-
      thing of worth in these words.

214   Thank you, Madeleine Thien and Rawi Hage, for the wandering conversations
      that led me to ponder the crafts we use, and the crafts we make.

215   Brianna Lei's *Butterfly Soup*, "if I was crossing the street and a car came barrel-
      ing toward me, I'm not sure I'd get out of the way."

215   Thank you to erin Khuê Ninh and Shireen Roshanravan, who guided this project
      from the beginning, and wrote in the introduction to its first publication, "high-
      risk behavior . . . trust a jury of readers not to convict?"

216   Thank you to David Chariandy, who gave feedback on an early draft of this book
      while we selfishly picked shells from a seafood tower.

224   After Gwendolyn Brooks and Ross Gay.

thank you to you the reader who is the same color as myself and that color is not blue or brown but purple purple my mother's favorite color purple the okra as it turns from red to green purple the bruise that fades from red to blue purple the not yet exposed blood that still discolors skin thank you to the reader who does not know they are purple but is nevertheless purple purple the sun setting sky purple the lowest energy frequency of light purple the moisture above a storm purple the shift when light creates dark thank you to you the reader who because you are purple you are not going to hurt yourself today thank you to the reader who is just for now turning purple purple the hazy neon sign that's on all day but only visible at night purple because it's there to say that it will never go away purple because resolution is a memoirist's game thank you to the purple reader you who keep yourself reminded that we are just flesh not yet exposed not yet decomposed the purple of he or she or them who will always be inside you like mice who keep you up at night with nibbles and scrapes who are both pests and pets thank you to the reader who knows it can feel too hard to be purple you who want to burst open your purple skin just to change its color you who want to shatter the purple sun before it can set thank you to the purple reader who is sometimes black and brown and yellow and red and blue and green you who have thought about all the ways that are easily available for you to do it without doing it thank you to the purple reader who has thought of eating cake just to push your insulin levels of showing the rage inside you to someone who will surely defend themselves of swallowing pills in a place where your body will never be found of traveling to some foreign country to fall off a cliff or get run over by a truck of getting drunk and pushing the gas pedal with your purple brick of a foot thank you to the purple reader who knows that if you did those things it would be a kindness because nobody would diagnose you and say that there's a pandemic among your people thank you to the purple reader who knows that if you did it that way no one in your family would ask what made you do it nor would they blame themselves thank you to the reader who has thought that if you did it just right you would be kindly forgotten as just an empty and invisible name I thank you purple reader because you were never tempted to own a gun not because of politics but because deep down you know that a pistol in your hands would be the worst way to protect yourself from yourself thank you purple reader for you are fast learning all the ways you can destroy yourself without doing damage to yourself or others thank you purple reader for today even though you may feel like you're not moving you will still lie down to watch the colors wash over the evening sky

bibliography

Against Me! "Paralytic States." #9 on *Transgender Dysphoria Blues*. Total Treble Music, 2014. Digital.

Against Me! "Transgender Dysphoria Blues." #1 on *Transgender Dysphoria Blues*. Total Treble Music, 2014. Digital.

Ahmed, Sara. "A Phenomenology of Whiteness." *Feminist Theory* 8, no. 49 (2007): 149–68. 159.

Alvar, Mia. *In the Country: Stories*. New York: Alfred A. Knopf, 2015. 94.

Anthony Bourdain: No Reservations. "Peru." Season 2, Episode 3. 44 min. Travel Channel. April 6, 2006.

Augustine of Hippo, Saint, and Sarah Ruden. *Confessions: A New Translation*. New York: Modern Library, 2017.

Baldwin, James. *The Fire Next Time*. New York: Knopf Doubleday, 2013. 33.

Baldwin, James. *Notes of a Native Son*. New York: Beacon Press, 1955. 84.

Berlant, Lauren. "Interview: Lauren Berlant." *ArtForum*, 2014. Accessed December 1, 2021. https://www.artforum.com /interviews/lauren-berlant-discusses-reading-with-and-her -recent-work-45109.

Bourdain, Anthony. *The Nasty Bits: Collected Varietal Cuts, Usable Trim, Scraps, and Bones*. New York: Bloomsbury, 2010. xi.

Brand, Dionne. *An Autobiography of the Autobiography of Reading*. Edmonton: University of Alberta Press, 2020. 8.

Buffett, Jimmy. "Margaritaville." #6 on *Changes in Latitudes, Changes in Attitudes*. ABC Records, 1977. Digital.

Butler, Judith. *Gender Trouble: Feminism and the Subversion of Identity*. New York: Routledge, 1999. 38.

Cha, Theresa Hak Kyung. *Dictee*. Berkeley: University of California Press, 2009. 4.

Chin, Marilyn. "Autumn Leaves." Poets.org. Accessed January 9, 2022. https://poets.org/poem/autumn-leaves.

Chingu: Friend. Directed by Kyŏng-tʻaek Kwak, O-sŏng Yu, Tong-gŏn Chang, et al. Seoul: Tŏksŭn Midiŏ, 2002.

Christian, Barbara. "The Race for Theory." *Cultural Critique* 6, no. 6 (1987): 51–63. 61.

Clark, Naomi. Consentacle: A Collaborative Card Game of Trust, Intimacy and Communication for Two Players—Human x Alien. Board Game Geeki. 2018. Accessed March 21, 2021. https://boardgamegeek.com/boardgame/166976/consentacle.

ContraPoints. "Archives: Gender Dysphoria." ContraPoints.com, 2020. Accessed December 7, 2022. https://www.contrapoints .com/transcripts/archives/gender-dysphoria.

ContraPoints. "Violence." ContraPoints, YouTube, 2017. Accessed December 8, 2021. https://www.youtube.com/watch?v=lmso VFCUN3Q.

ContraPoints. YouTube, February 6, 2021. https://www.youtube .com/c/contrapoints.

Deen, Mashuq Mushtaq, erin Khuê Ninh, Shireen Roshanravan, and Christopher B. Patterson. "#WeToo Reader." New Books Network, 2021. Accessed February 4, 2022. https://newbooks network.com/erin-khu%C3%AA-ninh-wetoo-reader-jaas-2021.

Du Bois, W. E. B., and Brent Hayes Edwards. *The Souls of Black Folk*. Oxford: Oxford University Press, 2007. 7.

Du Fu and David Hinton. *The Selected Poems of Tu Fu*. New York: New Directions, 2020.

Green Day. "Haushinka." #12 on *nimrod*. Reprise, 1997. Digital.

Green Day. "Platypus (I Hate You)." #8 on *nimrod*. Reprise, 1997. Digital.

Green Day. "Walking Contradiction." #14 on *Insomniac*. Reprise, 1995. Digital.

Guillermo, Kawika. *All Flowers Bloom*. Washington, DC: Westphalia Press, 2020.

Guillermo, Kawika. *Stamped: An Anti-travel Novel*. Washington, DC: Westphalia Press, 2018.

Hartman, Saidiya. *Wayward Lives, Beautiful Experiments: Intimate Histories of Social Upheaval*. New York: W. W. Norton, 2019. 21.

hooks, bell. *The Will to Change: Men, Masculinity, and Love*. New York: Washington Square Press, 2005. 18.

Hwang, David Henry, and Giacomo Puccini. *M. Butterfly*. New York: New American Library, 1989. 18.

Jay-Z. "Can I Live?" #8 on *Reasonable Doubt*. Roc-A-Fella, 1996. Digital.

Joyce, James, and Hans Walter Gabler. *Portrait of the Artist as a Young Man*. New York: Routledge, 2013. 199.

Kearney, Douglas. "Poem of the Week by Douglas Kearney." *Buffalo News*, 2015. Accessed December 6, 2022. https://buffalonews.com/lifestyles/poem-of-the-week-by-douglas-kearney/article_9e0a626f-5dfb-50a4-91c6-44364d1e8ebd.html.

Kim, Eunsong. "Petty Materialism: On Metaphor & Violence." *Michigan Quarterly Review* Online, 2020. Accessed February 19, 2022. https://sites.lsa.umich.edu/mqr/2020/12/petty-materialism-on-metaphor-violence/.

Kushner, Tony. *Angels in America: A Gay Fantasia on National Themes*. New York: Theatre Communications Group, 2003. 211.

Lei, Brianna. *Butterfly Soup*. Itch.io, 2017. Accessed May 1, 2020. https://brianna-lei.itch.io/butterfly-soup.

Lorde, Audre. *Zami; Sister Outsider; Undersong*. New York: Quality Paperback Book Club, 1993.

Marks, Laura. *Touch: Sensuous Theory and Multisensory Media*. Minneapolis: University of Minnesota Press, 2002.

Masahiro, Sugano, Anida Yoeu Ali, and Kosal Khiev, dirs. *Cambodian Son*. Studio Revolt, 2014.

Maximum Rocknroll. "Major Labels." *Maximum Rocknroll* no. 133, June. Archive.org, 1994. Accessed December 6, 2021. https://archive.org/details/mrr_133_con.

Mitski. "My Body's Made of Crushed Little Stars." #7 on *Puberty 2*. Dead Oceans, 2016. Digital.

Musser, Amber Jamilla. *Sensual Excess: Queer Femininity and Brown Jouissance*. New York: New York University Press, 2018. 167.

Nguyen Tan Hoang. *A View from the Bottom: Asian American Masculinity and Sexual Representation*. Durham, NC: Duke University Press, 2014. 154.

924 Gilman. "About." 924 Gilman, 2022. Accessed February 9, 2022. https://www.924gilman.org/about/.

Pardlo, Gregory. *Digest*. New York: Four Way Books, 2014. 4.

Patterson, Bill. *Search for True Discipleship in Church History*. Texas: Star Bible, 1989.

Pearl Jam. "Down." #3 on *Lost Dogs*. Epic Records, 2003. Digital.

Rancid. "Roots Radical." #3 on *. . . And Out Come the Wolves*. Epitaph Records, 1995. Digital.

Roshanravan, Shireen, and erin Khuê Ninh. "#WeToo: A Convening." *Journal of Asian American Studies* 24, no. 1 (2021): 1–8. 4.

Saunders, Patricia J. "Fugitive Dreams of Diaspora: Conversations with Saidiya Hartman." *Anthurium* 6, no. 1 (2008): 7.

Sedgwick, Eve Kosofsky. *A Dialogue on Love*. Boston: Beacon Press, 1999.

Sharif, Solmaz. "Force Visibility." Poets.org, 2016. Accessed August 18, 2020. https://poets.org/poem/force-visibility.

Sharif, Solmaz. "A Poetry of Proximity." *Kenyon Review* Online, 2014. Accessed June 9, 2022. https://kenyonreview.org/kr -online-issue/kenyon-review-credos/selections/sharif-credo/.

Sharpe, Christina. *In the Wake: On Blackness and Being*. Durham, NC: Duke University Press, 2016. 13.

Sontag, Susan. *Against Interpretation and Other Essays*. New York: Picador, 2001. 289.

Spivak, Gayatri, and Nazish Brohi. "Herald Exclusive: In Conversation with Gayatri Spivak." *Dawn*, 2014. Accessed February 28, 2022. https://www.dawn.com/news/1152482.

Springsteen, Bruce. "Born in the U.S.A." #3 on *Born in the U.S.A*. Columbia Records, 1984. Digital.

Tsing, Anna Lowenhaupt. *The Mushroom at the End of the World: On the Possibility of Life in Capitalist Ruins*. Princeton, NJ: Princeton University Press, 2015. 21.

Ward, Jesmyn. *Salvage the Bones: A Novel*. New York: Bloomsbury, 2012.

West, Kanye. "All of the Lights." #5 on *My Beautiful Dark Twisted Fantasy*. Def Jam, 2010. Digital.

Wu, Ellen D. *The Color of Success: Asian Americans and the Origins of the Model Minority*. Princeton, NJ: Princeton University Press, 2014. 1.